THE HAPPINESS RECIPE

THE HAPPINESS RECIPE

Discover the
unique ingredients
you need to thrive

IESHA DELUNE

Email: hello@ieshadelune.com

IeshaDelune.com

ISBN: 978-1-6451-6655-9 (paperback)

ISBN: 978-1-6451-6337-4 (electronic)

Dedication

Contents

Introduction

What is happiness anyway? This is a question I have asked at the beginning of a lot of my interactive workshops and the answers vary widely. We use the same word to describe everything from joyful glee to contented satisfaction. For some, happiness means feeling delighted and in high spirits and for others it is more the absence of stress, and the presence of peace in mind and body.

Whenever I am asked to define happiness, I prefer to come out of that word, due to the diverse interpretations, and introduce the concept of congruence. When I use this word, I am speaking of the following state of being: your mind, body, heart and soul, thinking, feeling and acting in alignment with the truth of who *you* are. What I have found is that all human beings have a Happiness Recipe and it's unique to them. Genuine, authentic happiness is the natural and effortless by-product of living in this alignment.

When you *seek* happiness by doing things, most likely things that seem to be making other people happy, you can often be moving further and further away from what is actually right for you, as the unique being that you are.

It is getting more and more common to be stressed out by regular, daily life and to experience anxiety, depression and mood swings. To me, it seems like a mental and emotional epidemic and there are millions of people believing that how they think and feel is the result of forces outside of their own control. I am a passionate advocate of personal empowerment! You do have the ability to change the way you think and feel and therefore produce changes in the chemistry of your body.

So, stress is on the rise, and there are ever-increasing options of the best way to "manage" this and also huge growth in ways to distract yourself from the core issues. Interestingly, for those already on the path of intentional self-improvement, some of the most popular distractions are promoted as "stress management".

Here's the thing: Your stress is not meant to be *managed*. It is feedback that something, or many things, need to change!

There is a sense of entitlement for some, that great relationships, success and goal-achievement happens for the 'lucky' or the 'already-wealthy' and that it should be freely given out if someone is a 'nice' person. There are also many people who have decided they are somehow so flawed, that the natural process of actions, creating reactions, cannot work for them to create change. I appreciate that there are more challenging circumstances for some, and greater ease for others. That said, both of these perceptions embody total disempowerment. There are also many types of treatment and therapy that perpetuate disempowerment, blame and keep nourishing the idea that one's mental and emotional health is not in our own hands. This, perhaps, cultivates the *understanding* of why one feels the way they do (your parents, your health, your genes, the 'the state of the world') but plots no path forward to thinking, feeling or acting differently.

There are immeasurable numbers of people working in jobs that are not a match for their values, that do not utilise their capacity or make use of their potential. There are countless people in relationships that do not honour them, in circumstances that make their heart shrink with the unfelt-joy they are capable of. There are multitudes of people who have settled for dissatisfaction, frustration and lack of meaningful fulfilment and decided that it's 'normal' to feel that way. It's not, it's completely unnecessary! Our bodies are designed to be living in emotional states that range from neutral to happy. This is how your physical self has the energy for high-quality thinking and action, digestion, fertility and sleep. In neutral to happy states our bodies engage, daily, in the routine healing, maintenance and repair that keeps us healthy, with energy and vitality for life. Ongoing stress compromises the body's ability to do these things, as it's acting in the immediate moment and mobilising all that talent to fight, hide or run from danger. When the danger you perceive is continuing, because you're not winning the fight or successfully escaping, there is no opportunity to completely turn off the stress response. This is why your whole being is giving you feedback that something needs to change! These are not natural feelings, unless you're being chased by a predator. It's not 'just the way it is'. It's not 'modern life', but your response to it.

All in all, it boils down to two things. Firstly, a disconnect from our authentic selves. So many people are all striving for the exact same thing as everyone else and expecting happiness to be the result, rather than having curiosity about our personal preferences. You have a uniqueness that makes you who you are. When we deny that, it's as stressful as a tropical fruit tree trying to grow near the freezing cold poles (there'd be feedback that it wasn't thriving!) Secondly, we are lacking in knowledge of what to do with our feelings. Supressing them creates more stress in the long-term. Feeling them in loops with no escape also puts pressure on the body. What's needed is, what I call 'Emotional Digestion', acknowledgment, feeling, processing and healthy movement through the experience and out the other side into wisdom. In this book I am going to show you ways of connecting with your truth. Not mine, or anyone else's but your own. This is going to resolve that disconnection and give you tools you can use for the rest of your life, to live wholeheartedly as your magnificent self. I'm going to teach you how to listen to the feedback your body is giving you and ways to respond to it that will create life-long, positive transformations. We will also be learning about Emotional Digestion and ways of implementing this into your life. Think of this journey as a deepening and revealing of the truth of Beautiful You, rather than trying to get somewhere.

At the time of writing this book, I am 43 years old. I have been on my own journey with the tools for self-awareness, healing and empowerment since I was 19. I began studying and using various modalities of healing and change-work, supporting clients from age 22, and adding tools to my kit of personal empowerment and evolution. This study continues to date because I love to learn and grow and has thus far ranged from massage, Reiki and qi gong, through to holistic counselling, neurolinguistic programming, meditation, mindfulness, to personal and professional coaching. My qualifications and skill-set are broad and have always ranged through the areas of mind, body and energy. After working with and for others in wellbeing centres around full-time work in other areas, I opened my own private practice when I was 28, which was in 2004. I bring it all together now as a Transformational Life Coach, keynote presenter and workshop facilitator. In teaching, speaking and in my one-on-one work, I am supporting people to embrace their uniqueness, listen to their *own* wisdom and implement authenticity so that what inspires their mind, body, heart and soul is reflected in their personal and professional lives. Profound self-acceptance and healthy happiness are just two of the very common results.

In 2013, I published my first book, "The Answer – 42 days of connecting with your Authentic Personal Power". I was propelled by an unquenchable passion to share with people an instruction manual for how to use their innate equipment of mind, body and energy to feel in control of their lives and connected with their personal power in a genuine and heartfelt way. I knew, and wanted to share, that people already have the raw resources they need to thrive, that they could stop looking outside of themselves, and just learn how to make their innate resources work to build new, profound and empowered life experiences.

In the years between that book and the one you're now reading, I realised a heartbreaking truth that had not captured my attention previously. There are so many people on this path of self-improvement, who have learned mind-tools to create positive mental states, how to nutritionally nourish their body for radiant health and meditation practices to clear their energy and they use this power to forcibly plant themselves in life circumstances where they could *never* thrive. They ignore the feedback their body is giving them; the stress that they decide needs to be 'managed', rather than listened to; the flatness that they ignore with distractions, stimulants, or relaxants; the dissatisfaction that they blame on others or on themselves. The belief that there's something else they need to 'fix' or 'get over'. The idea that they're permanently broken and just have to make the best they can with the pieces that are left.

The truth is that you are not broken and you do not need fixing, you may however need some *knowing*. In this book, I am going to teach you how to uncover the powerful essence of You. The core of your beautiful self. From this knowing, you will have unmissable and completely personalised guidance for the way forward.

In my coaching work, we always begin with the foundation of you. I will not support someone to create an elaborate extension on top of a foundation that isn't honouring of themselves. No builder would invest their time and energy to extend a house on questionable foundations, without some serious investigation and, as the builder of your own life, I suggest you don't either. This miracle of holistic engineering we are all living in, our own body, is giving us moment by moment feedback on how aligned we are in our lives. Our bodies let us know when we are tired, what people we feel safe and comfortable with, what is stressful and what is inspiring and stimulating. The wonderful thing is that this feedback is personalised – direct from your being to you. What I find enlivening may bore you silly, that's why my body isn't ever going to be telling you what's important and values-aligned to you. What I find stressful and totally incongruent may be the activity that brings you purpose, meaning and soul-deep satisfaction to your life.

That is why this book is a personal discovery, between you and you, not the manual of what works for me or anybody else. And, with this kind of understanding, you can update your Happiness Recipe over time. As you enter new ages and stages of your life and your needs, values and priorities change. Your Happiness Recipe is a living thing, like a part of nature, that I invite you to know and update for the rest of your life.

Your unique Happiness Recipe consists of several key ingredients, all of which will be explored through the chapters in this book.

- Understanding the foundations of your personal power. This means that you have total clarity around the parts of your life that are totally within your control.

- Processing your emotions, moving through to wisdom. This ends ongoing, repetitive patterns that keep you from having a satisfying and joyful life.

- Becoming aware of your *unique* care label and using it to guide your choices. Over years of teaching The Happiness Recipe workshop, there have never been two participants with the exact same elements on their care label. Knowing yours allows you to care for yourself and utilise more of your potential.

- Healthy connection with your body so as to correctly interpret its feedback.

- Knowing your core values and using them to guide your priorities and actions.

The concepts and tools I'll be teaching you have changed the lives of those who have made use of them. They have been developed through my own painful and joyful life experiences and honed through teaching and supporting others. It represents the cream of the crop, harvested from over two decades of working with clients, learning and implementation. I share stories of clients (with names changed) to demonstrate application of these tools. To support you in getting the most from this time together, I am inviting you to participate in a journal process throughout the book. I promise that when used, these tools will empower you to change your life for the better!

You are living inside a miracle of physiological engineering. A magnificent fusion of mind, body and energy, with all the tools you need to awaken your authentic uniqueness and empower your life; to be living in satisfying alignment with all that you truly are. The real you, underneath all those well-practiced behaviours and the roles you play by default or through some sort of "this is how it is and I just have to accept it" programming that hasn't been your heartfelt choice. You are here on Earth not just to survive, but to THRIVE and I'm going to show you how!

Are you ready to take the reins of your life and benefit from this dynamic and powerful shift in perspective?

Are you ready to know what steps to take? And then, moment by moment, step by step to take them?

Now that you know what's possible and that this recipe is already inside of you, waiting to be unwrapped, please don't wait to get started receiving from this book. If one of your well-practiced behaviours is starting 'later', then let's break that pattern now. If it's self-criticism, then you've just learned enough to add *more* to the criticism repertoire! It is my deep wish that you start to see the strength of your heart, know the wisdom of your body and the power you have in all the circumstances in your life, if you know how to listen, ask yourself the right questions and take actions. Your daily life is filled with actions, you don't have to do *more*, you'll just learn how to put your time, energy and focus into what honours you, rather than draining you or creating more of the same.

So, let's dive right in. Why wait? Your truest essence is calling you forward to be living with congruence and the happiness that enlivens your body and being.

Foundation Concepts

"Beauty begins the moment you decide to be yourself"

Coco Chanel

There are some perception-shifts that I want to move through with you, before we step into the rest of this book. I want to help you establish the most useful frame of mind possible, so as to support the most positive transformation possible. As I'm sure you already know, the way in which we move into a new experience can dramatically affect the results. For example, if you are to be speaking at a public event with other speakers and you go into this experience with the unshakable belief that you will be the least talented and most boring person there, you'll already be feeling future embarrassment before you've even said a word. If you go into the same experience with a lot of practice, you really know your topic and you cultivate your presentation with the passion you feel for it, the feelings going in will be different. It won't give you instant confidence as a public presenter, because only lots of public presenting can do that, but you will go into it more openly, feeling more confident and prepared, not embarrassed before you've even begun. Embedded in this example is one of the lessons within this book. You have the lead role in changing how you feel, by putting time and effort into shifting your thinking and actions. We will get very specifically into how to do this later on, but for now, just know it's possible. We want to move into these lessons with the most fertile soil for your understanding and growth, so it's important to invite in a new lens to modify and enhance these lessons and their digestion and implementation.

Perception shift number 1 – An invitation for curiosity.

Judgement gets a bad rap in the world of self-improvement. So many clients and students start with the firm belief that they need to get less judgmental, about themselves and others. I have two things to say about this.

Firstly, not all judgement is bad. We use our judgement, based on our lifetime of learning, to do daily things like safely cross roads. We need our judgment to notice who brings out the best (and the worst) in us. Both interviewer and potential employee use judgement in the interviewing process, to decide on whether there is a good fit between organisation, job role and the personalities in the workplace; to determine whether there will be synergy or disharmony. We use judgement when we smell milk that's nudging up to its used by date – is this going to be fresh enough to use? Judgement as a noun is defined as the ability to make considered decisions or come to sensible conclusions, and it is a wonderful skill to have. So firstly, let's loosen up our judgement around the word 'judgement'.

Now, not all judgement is benign. Self-judgement can hold back our progress and development and make life so much more miserable than it needs to be. Judgement of others can poison relationships, killing them unnecessarily. Similarly, but in the opposite direction, turning judgement inwards and blaming yourself, rather than judging others, can have you staying in harmful relationships. The tools you'll be learning in this book will really help you to know and feel which situations and circumstances are right for you.

Secondly, it is so much easier to stop a damaging habit if you add another, more positive habit in its place. This is the moment where I am going to invite you to enter into the new perspective of curiosity.

When we enter into the state of openness to learning and knowing ourselves in a new way, it further loosens harmful patterns of judgment. When we ask, "I wonder why this is?" or "what's really going for me here?" it creates a useful, exploratory kind of thinking that is open to finding new answers.

Perception shift number 2 – You are not broken and you do not need fixing. You may however need some knowing.

In Hans Christian Anderson's story, The Ugly Duckling, we are introduced to a little 'duck' that never belonged and its painful journey of rejections and aloneness. In the end of the story, it sees a flock of such beautiful birds that it just wants to be near them even though, based on its previous life experiences, it expects to be pecked to death. The 'duck' is willing to go to its death, just to be with the beauty it could see in those other birds. In being drawn to this beauty it is able to truly see itself for the first time, as a beautiful swan, and belong in this herd that looked so wondrous from its painful beginnings. Clarissa Pinkola used this story in her book, "Women Who Run with the Wolves", to discuss the importance of belonging. I bring it to your attention to let you know that it does not matter how much therapy you get, personal development you do, how much you 'work' on yourself, you will not find the kind of soul-deep happiness that you're yearning for if you are a swan, trying to be a duck and fit into a world of other ducks. You'll always be *not good enough* for them and yourself. The real truth is that you can never be 'not good enough' at being you. You can be not good enough at being someone else, and thank goodness because you only have the blueprint and innate guidance for being *you*. On some level, most unhappiness is a disconnect with self. Often, we are trying to be what we've admired, or what our family or society has indicated is 'right' and 'good'. Or perhaps what you're choosing is the logical next step and you're just on that road, not doing a lot of curious self-inquiry. So many of the divorced clients I've worked with actually knew on, or leading up to, their wedding day that the relationship wasn't right. Imagine the time and pain that can be saved by learning to really *know* yourself and have the tools to listen to your knowing and act on it.

So let's start with getting curious about, "What fuel am I using to move through my life?"

Take off your armour in the privacy of your relationship with yourself. Put aside all the well-practiced behaviours and the roles you play with and for others. Let's begin this journey with a solid foundation of curious self-inquiry.

Am I fuelling each day with a propulsion to be better, based on the premise that I am not already wonderfully *enough*?

Am I fuelling my days with a knowing that I am worthy and deserving of happiness and I'm on this life-adventure of discovering who I am, what I value, what inspires and delights me and the ways I want to share that?

Please know that I understand life isn't all about swirling around mountain tops, hills alive with sound and love. I know, and have experienced myself, many times, how hard it is to pick yourself back up and keep moving when you're depleted, exhausted and experiencing bone-deep devastation and sadness. I know that most of us have had destabilising, debilitating, painful experiences of loss and heartbreaking disappointments. I have supported clients who are grieving the loss of children, partners and other loved ones to accident or suicide, survivors of rape and other horrific assaults and almost fatal domestic abuse. I am not a stranger to life's darker and heavier feelings. I promise that I am not making light of life's smorgasbord of experiences, telling you to get a spring in your step and it will all magically disappear. Some of life is tripe and some is sticky date pudding (and we're all so different that the appetising option there for some of us will be different). We will move further into and through navigating these times in the later chapters. For now, please accept the invitation to be curious about your healing, to be open for the beginnings of change and to fuel these changes with a deep knowing that there is a part of you, your essence, that leads you to books like these and that knows it's possible for you to feel better.

When we embark on any evolution of self with the premise that 'life will be better when I fix this about myself' you will, on some level, always be tracking for what needs fixing. Or, even worse, you'll experience a total shift that's wonderfully freeing and decide it was just "one layer of the onion" and now you need to find the next layer to be fixed! You do not need to be fixed! You are already magnificent and extremely powerful! In the words of Abraham-Hicks, "you are so powerful you can choose bondage" [the state of being a slave]. What we will be doing in this book is supporting your self-discovery so that you can see your magnificence and use your power to cultivate a congruent life. When I use the word congruent, I mean that your body, heart, mind and soul are all in alignment with your values and priorities. This is the key to deep happiness and fulfilment. It is also the way to have the most positive and profound impact on your own health and the world around you. In this space, you will have goals and plans but this is fundamentally different to the idea that you need fixing. Let me explain with an analogy: learning to drive.

If you are learning to drive based on the premise that you need to fix this horrible flaw that you can't drive and until you can you'll be absolutely certain of your 'not good enough' status, it will probably have some elements like these: you'll compare yourself to people who are already licenced drivers and fall short in your comparison. You'll bring a lot of stress and pressure to your learning and focus on what you didn't do correctly – I stalled (what an idiot), I forgot to check my mirrors (that will be an instant fail, I'll never get there, I'll fail my test), why is this taking so long? It doesn't take this long for other people! I have trouble learning! This is so hard for me!

Imagine it this way instead. You are learning to drive because you desire the freedom, flexibility and independence of being licenced. You fuel your actions with the knowing that you are capable of learning and curiosity around how long it will take (but no timeline pressure). Just like you've learned to walk, talk, effectively use the toilet and loads of other practical life skills that you were not born with, you will also learn this new thing with the practise of trial and correction. And, just like those other skills, there are some things you learn faster than others, and other things that it takes you longer to get a confident grasp on. You know that you get better at what you practice and you practise at the things that are important to you. You'll be saying to yourself: "I'm going to get there and I'm going to *love* driving!"

I know you can feel the difference between the two approaches. Let us welcome in the fuel of curiosity and the shift in perception that we will improve in the practising of things that are important to us. If happiness is important to you and you're willing to dive in and get to really know the true essence of you, and take action from that knowing fuelled with care-based curiosity, you will soon be living a positively different future.

Let's begin a new life-book, starting with a fresh, blank page, and get curious about who you are. What are your likes and dislikes? What enlivens you? What creates real happiness in your heart? And, what do you really need to thrive?

Perception shift number 3 – You have an individual care label.

Human beings are not one size fits all. Not in clothing, not in our values, preferences and priorities and certainly not in our inspirations. This is a wonderful thing! In societies, we need all different types of people to accomplish the synergy of a well-functioning community.

This book is a discovery process of your entire Happiness Recipe, an important ingredient of which is your own care label. I invite you to think about this care label, like what you find on a clothing garment, that instructs you on the do's and don'ts for washing and drying. Or, like the care label on a purchased plant that shows you the right temperature range, shade and sun requirements and type of nutrients needed for optimal growth. You too have a care label for your own optimal living. Ours, however, are not neatly printed on our skin which stimulates the need for self-inquiry.

In the whole of Chapter 5, we will be exploring your care label in detail. I introduce the idea now as I will be referencing it through the book. Also, because it is a really important shift in perception that's required to allow in and digest the lessons we will be working through. When our concepts and plans for happiness are based on what someone else has got, that seems to be making them happy, you are doomed to keep repeating unhappy lessons. Your care label is specific to you. Your own body and being is giving you real-time feedback on how in-alignment you are with your own care label. When you learn your care label and give yourself permission to be your full self, giving yourself the conditions *you* need to thrive, it benefits yourself and every person you touch lives with.

Perception shift number 4 – How you are isn't fixed and permanent, but ever changing.

I need to bust the idea that your emotional state of being is somehow fixed and permanent. You cannot *be* depressed, in the same way that you cannot *be* the flu. You can be knocked around by it, destabilised out of your usual capabilities by it, but it is an experience you are having, in a moment (or over several moments) of time. It is the result of a series of elements and *all* of these elements are in a constant state of change. Both our body and our beings are living verbs. They are perpetually in a state of motion, creating health (or its opposite) and responding to your internal and external environments. The way we frame up and describe our emotional states and physiological experiences really determine whether we are doomed to the experience forever, always looking for its reappearance when we are having a reprieve, or whether we are open to positive and life-long change. When a client says to me "I have anxiety" and they honestly mean it, in the same way as they would say, "I have arms" there is no real hope for and belief in change. Instead, they are looking for managing a symptom that they believe will be a constant life-companion. Perpetuating this way of looking at emotional states is disastrous to one's empowerment, self-esteem, hope for the future and also horrifically incorrect. It also sets up a self-fulfilling prophesy. In the words of Henry Ford, "whether you think you can, or think you can't, you're right".

What you believe will directly impact the effort and commitment you make to solutions. How much ongoing focus and energy you put into solutions will directly impact the quality of your results. These results then feedback into your belief. Because life is in a constant state of motion, nothing is really fixed and your attitude, expectations and beliefs play a major role in the outcomes you are producing with your efforts, or lack thereof.

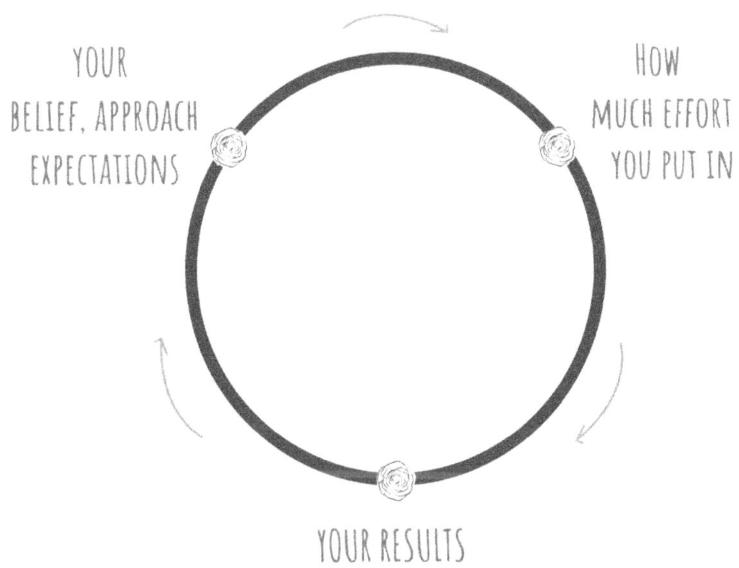

Let's start with your physical body. If you are a forty year old who has decided that aches and pains are a normal part of aging, you're not likely to put effort into understanding the feedback your body is giving you. If that is not your belief, you may begin to include some stretches in your morning or throughout your day. Your cells are dividing, right now. The skin cells you can see are not the ones that were there a month ago. The blood that's pumping through your veins is not the same moving liquid as a few months ago. This is why you can safely donate blood several times a year. I know from my own shifts and changes in diet and lifestyle what a difference it makes when I fuel my body with nourishing ingredients and the right movement.

I have also had countless experiences of working with clients, alongside other health professionals, improving their mental and emotional state. I facilitate the mental and emotional transformation and other practitioners offer the more physical and nutritional support. I have witnessed irrefutable improvements in energy levels, eye clarity, healthy weight adjustments, clearing of skin, normalisation and uplifted quality of mind and mood when the body is getting what it needs, how and when it needs it, for optimal physical functioning. The mind, body, emotions and energy levels are not truly separable. Even modern, Western medicine acknowledges that stress is physically damaging and that exercise is a useful way to lift depressive symptoms. This is why the word holistic is getting used so often now. And it is why my company is called Wholistic Vitality [I use the 'W' because I like the mental vision of whole, rather than hole]. What we choose to ingest, on a daily basis, has a daily effect on what proteins are activated in our DNA. What we ingest includes everything that passes through our mouths and also what we watch, read, focus on and who we spend our time with.

Now let's look at your internal, mental and emotional environment. What you think about creates a lot of what you're feeling about. Your day to day, surface thinking generates the mood you're in. If you think now of one of the happiest moments of your life and really allow yourself to go there, replay the words and pictures inside your mind, you will feel the upliftment echoing from that past. I have seen so many clients who feel joyless, give themselves to this exercise and have happy tears in their eyes from the wonderful memories of their lives. We didn't have a time machine, we just went there in their thinking and gave time and energy to those pockets of memory that recreate joy. For those who, thus far, haven't experienced that kind of emotion, I take them forwards. Perhaps they long to be a parent, so we go forwards to holding their new baby, who looks up at them with the kind of loving adoration that melts the heart of every loving parent. Whatever the dream is, if it's congruent with their truest self, there is emotion in the imagining of it when they give thought to its fruition.

Generally, in order to have ongoing negative emotion, thought-time and energy will need to be given to the kind of thinking that supports negative emotions. What we think about all day long will be creating our feelings and our reactions all day long, too.

Our surface thinking has a huge impact on how we are feeling each and every moment. We also have unconscious patterning, the deep beliefs that are so ingrained they are not questioned. These shift as you do work on yourself to break your unconscious mould and create life-long change. It is possible to have unconscious patterning that believes in your worthiness or lack thereof; programming that has decided, before you even begin, that you will fail or that no one will really care. We really do create possibilities based on who we've decided we are, our limitations and our capacity. It is one of the most delightful parts of my work to see the changes that begin to effortlessly take place when clients begin to change their unconscious patterning. The world of opportunities opens up and they are now limited only by their own efforts.

Take a moment now to imagine the impact of your external environment. By this, I mean all of your circumstances that are outside of your own body; all of your relationships, your daily activities, your work in the world and your environment. We will be going into all of these through this book but for now, enter the understanding that what you do with your time and who you surround yourself with, has a huge impact on your happiness.

Your relationships with others are, likewise, not fixed. When you assume that others are 'just the way they are', and that won't be changing, and that you are 'just the way you are', you're doing the whole interaction a great disservice. The word 'relationship' is the nominalisation of the verb, 'to relate'. What does it mean for you, when you say, "I can really relate to them"? Generally, to have that feeling of connection, you need to have some rapport and understanding. There is a whole chapter in my first book, "The Answer" called "Empowered Communication – How to own your 'stuff' and still talk about how you feel" which provides a structure in sharing feelings without blaming the other person. In this book I want to reiterate that you are responsible for how honestly you communicate and how deeply you allow someone to know you. You are also responsible for how you choose to listen in your relationships. In reality, communication in important relationships could easily be its own book. In Chapter 3, Cause and Effect, we will be exploring relationship dynamics, sharing and listening.

All of these areas of your existence, your physical body, your thoughts and programs, your emotions, relationships, daily activities, priorities and interactions are changeable with decisions you are able and capable of making. They are not permanent and fixed!

So these are our foundation concepts. You have stepped into the journey of uncovering your Happiness Recipe. It's always been there and now you're creating time and space to find it and work with it to create congruence and therefore authentic and lasting happiness in your life. If you can be curious about your personal recipe and open to it being unique to you, it will be possible to fuel this journey of self-inquiry with the kind of excitement we might feel when we go on a few fabulous dates and we're thinking, "Oooh, I really want to get to know you!". Developing a curiosity and care-based relationship with yourself is a wonderful fuel for this process.

The Two Types of Happiness

There are two types of happiness: Surface Happiness and Soul-Deep Happiness. I'm going to introduce them to you as if they are totally separate, for the ease of explanation, but they are deeply intertwined and both dramatically improved by knowing and following your Happiness Recipe.

We will first look into Surface Happiness, as the rest of the book is dedicated to the tools for cultivating the soul-deep happy, values-aligned experience of yourself and the world around you.

Surface Happiness refers to your state of mind and mood, right at the top and outer-most experience of yourself, moment to moment. Like if you are doing something you enjoy or spending time with someone who brings out the best in you. Soul-Deep Happiness is the result of your body, heart, mind and soul being in congruent alliance. When your environment, both internally and externally, accepts and supports who you truly are.

Surface Happiness is fleeting because it is experienced in the moment, based on what is going on right in that moment, and needs to be generated in an ongoing way if you're not soul-deep happy. Because it is generated by what is happening for you, right now, it will come and go based on what is happening for you right now or what you are focusing on mentally, right now. For example, it is possible to be in relationships that drain you, work that doesn't align with your values and be struggling with low energy from poor health but have a catch up with a friend that's filled with laughs and the kind of meaningful connection that creates a Surface Happiness. I call these moments, "soul food" and they are wonderful and necessary. That said, the happiness is experienced in the moment, but not sustainable long-term due to the deeper circumstances of your life. You may find that shortly after arriving back home, into the routines and behaviour patterns of your 'normal' life, that it only takes one comment to have you right back at the deflated feeling you had before that fun catch up.

Surface Happiness is often created with a shift in the body's chemistry. For example, we can generate Surface Happiness through exercise, which releases endorphins into the bloodstream. We can develop Surface Happiness by learning how to be more masterful with our minds, our internal dialog and the way we frame up and perceive the world. In other words, by working on our habitual thought patterns and default assumptions. Much of my book, "The Answer", shared very effective tools for achieving this. There are also many other books on this topic so I won't dedicate a lot of time to it in this one.

Based on your overall Happiness Recipe, there will be a variety of actions that will generate Surface Happiness for you. Here is a short list of some of the common ones: exercise that raises your heart rate, yoga, tai chi, qi gong. Positive thinking affirmations, especially if you can generate the feelings relating to your new thinking. Focusing on goals and plans that you feel great about and taking action in areas you feel confident in. Day dreaming about wonderful things. Shifting out of a negative headspace by reminding yourself of what is good in your life, feeling gratitude for all that you have. Being kind to others, being generous with your time, money, energy or efforts. Giving to a charity and spending money on something that you've wanted. Getting dressed up and feeling great in what you're wearing. Making love or having enjoyable sex. Changing environments, in the short term by leaving the room you're in and doing something else or, in the longer term by going on a holiday or moving to a new location. Gardening or being outside in nature. Walking, dancing, singing, creating, meditation, mindfulness. Spending time with wonderful friends, inspiring people or having time alone. Self-care, cuddles with someone you love and feel safe with, being pleasantly surprised, being around couples, friends or family who truly love each other.

Cultivating Surface Happiness through reverse engineering.

The following is an exercise I have used for many years and for a variety of reasons. It is very useful if you feel that you are rarely, if ever, happy and have no idea what makes you feel good. This is a very self-fulfilling way of thinking and feeling. Remember, what you believe and expect directly impact the effort you will choose to put in. I am yet to work long-term with anyone who doesn't shift this very damaging perception and realise its inherent untruth. Our minds can be very dedicated to certain self-perceptions so in doing this on your own, you'll need to watch out for that and call yourself on your own misperceptions. Once you realise that even one self-managed activity cultivates a mood improvement, you can begin to let that old pattern of thinking go. This exercise is also very useful for people who experience bouts of low quality of mind or mood. In that heavy place, that I call the 'blurk', it can be very challenging to imagine feeling better.

Perhaps you're in a pretty good mood most of the time but you don't know what it is that creates that mood because it just 'is' and you've never thought about it. Having clarity on the activities that provide Surface Happiness is wonderfully empowering, regardless of how regularly you have felt happy up until now.

Journal invitation:

1. Think about some of the happiest moments of your life. It can be just a single moment that captured your awareness and felt wonderful or it can be over hours of time. Go into those memories, ask yourself the following questions and write what comes to you:

   a) What was happening circumstantially?

   b) Were you alone or with others? If with others, who were you with and what was it about them that contributed?

   c) What kind of thoughts are you thinking?

   d) What were you doing with your body? Were you sitting, walking, lying down, or something else?

   e) What were you looking at, hearing, touching, tasting, feeling and sensing?

If your life, thus far, hasn't had a lot happy times, then we can expand this exercise to what has created the emotional and mental states of neutral to good. These things don't have to create joyful excitement. Perhaps they are the moments of reprieve from what you usually experience. When have you felt the most peaceful? What times in your life have been more okay than others? Recall those times and go through questions a)-e).

2. What kinds of things do you naturally do and choose when you're in a good place? A happy mood? Having a good time? What kinds of thoughts are you having? What are you focusing on?

   For me, when I'm in a happy mood, I just naturally sing a lot. I also want to go out for walks, regardless of the weather, because it feels so beautiful to breathe in the fresh air and move my body. I tend to feel very grateful for the beauty in my surroundings and the freedoms in my life

Give yourself the freedom to write what comes, regardless of whether it would be on anyone else's list. It does not need to be identified whether these are Surface Happiness or Soul-Deep Happiness elements of your life. They will intertwine regardless.

3. Make a list of at least ten thoughts, actions or experiences that feel good for you.

***

Now that you have your answers you can use them as a tool to reverse engineer your mood. If you're feeling a bit surface-blurky, instead of happy, choose some things you've identified through these questions and do them. The things we quite naturally do when we're in a good space will, quite naturally, engender a better-feeling mood, even when we begin them from a lower quality of mood.

I will use my example of singing and walking as natural activities birthed from feelings of happiness. Let's imagine I am having a tough week. I've had five nights of interrupted sleeping because one of my children has a cold and something I was really looking forward to was postponed. I take myself out for a walk, in nature, breathe deep and take my mind to what I'm seeing, not focusing on what's going on at home and the details of this postponement, but on the sounds of the birds and the wind in the trees. The feel of my body's movement. I quite naturally slip into gratitude for my beautiful surroundings and my body's ability to move. If I start singing a song I love, or creating a new melody and lyrics as I'm moving along, my whole being will start feeling better. It doesn't matter how resistant I may have felt leaving the house, how convinced I was that I wasn't in the mood or there wasn't time for this walk. That singing and walking, breathing and appreciating nature is a sure-fire way for me to connect with my deeper resources and I am always better at easily resolving whatever was an issue before I left the house. Walking and singing has worked for me if I was taking a twenty-minute walk in an industrial area or through a forest. If you look, nature is everywhere and dandelions coming through cement footpaths always make me smile about natures enduring strength.

Singing and positive thinking have gone together for me for a very long time. It's why I've created albums of Sing Your Affirmation tracks. Music has many wonderful, uplifting benefits for our brains, and lyrics bypass conscious resistance and allow us to feel things that aren't really happening. Have a look through all of your answers and see if there are some elements that will work well together. Write down some ideas of those combinations. Next time you feel a bit low, you can actively choose to lift your mood, using what you've just written down. This lift will provide some Surface Happiness relief and also give you more energy for any problem solving that's required. I often think of the well-known quote of Albert Einstein's, "We can't solve problems by using the same kind of thinking we used when we created them". This shift in your mood will enhance your ability to think creatively about solutions, along with feeling better in the moment.

Some of the things you've got on your list may end up being ingredients for that deeper, authentic and sustainable, Soul-Deep Happiness. Often these kinds of activities can stimulate that deeper essence of You to evaluate what is working for you and what you need to move on from, and in that way also create and arouse the energy for positive and life-changing action. As I said, they do intertwine. Here's a couple of examples:

Going out dancing with friends could be in total values

alignment and a natural symptom of Soul-Deep Happiness for someone who's care label includes fun exercise and social time. It could also be a temporary reprieve from life circumstances that are demeaning, draining or even dangerous. Either way, if you enjoy going out and dancing with your friends, this is a great activity for you! I'm highlighting the differences because temporary distractions will create a temporary shift in the short-term but will not *solve* ongoing life disharmonies.

Another example would be having a regular practice of an activity like yoga or qi gong. In the moment, any activity combining focused, conscious breath and physical movement, has the power to create inner and outer harmony. As a student and teacher of qi gong for over ten years and a student of yoga for over twenty years, I have experienced this first hand in countless people. For me, these practices penetrated my emotional depths, highlighted incongruencies and opened space for deep healing in my internal environment. What they didn't do was teach me how to practically deal with this more-connected me, in the relationships I had started from a place of less self-esteem. They created an undeniable knowing that I was unfulfilled but didn't teach me how to communicate effectively and be able to set and hold healthy boundaries.

Please know that both types of happiness have real value. Those temporary shifts into a happier state of being are wonderful to invest time into. That said, I want to explain the danger of believing that these two types of happiness are the same thing.

Some of the most cheerful and Surface Happy people I've ever worked with are, underneath, the saddest and least fulfilled of all. They're often very intuitive and respond to this inner-knowing of their unrealised potential by investing in more and more Surface Happiness or that previously-mentioned distortion of ongoing 'fixing' of themselves. It is possible, through using only the tools of Surface Happiness, to keep your head and heart way above deeper traumas and dysfunctions in your life and never face the issues in a way that creates resolution and the resulting freedom. In fact, using only Surface Happiness, without the self-worth that makes giving to others synergistic, you can give and give to your own depletion and exhaustion, all the while training those around you that there are no repercussions to behaving in a way that actually hurts. I have worked with so many of these types of givers, that use their personal development tools for Surface Happiness to experience premature healing and forgiveness (it's still on the surface), kindness and compassion that leads to giving *even more* into relationships devoid of respect, honour or care.

I also see many clients that hover around the edges of their potential, with enough Surface Happiness that they're not stimulating the bravery for change. They often blame the down times, where their inner self is whispering that they're capable of more, on hormones, sleep levels, hangovers or the idea that down-times are 'normal'. They keep on doing what they're doing, because it's okay, not stimulating or really making the difference they could make, but it's okay and 'that's life' and wanting or expecting more is a delusion of grandeur and therefore unrealistic.

I absolutely loved the priceless wisdom shared by Bronnie Ware in her book, "The Top Five Regrets of the Dying – A Life Transformed by the Dearly Departing" and I highly recommend that you read it. We will be accessing some of her wisdom here but that does not replace what you will receive from reading the whole. Bronnie's book began as a blog article of the same name and over three million people read it before her book was written. Enormous numbers of people contacted her about the article, connecting with the theme. It speaks to the deep part in all of us, the soul-deep part of us that knows our time as this person, in this lifetime, is mortal and therefore limited. From her time caring for dying people and all of the feedback she has received, she's realised "just how much we all have in common, despite cultural differences". I will list the top five regrets and please allow yourself a moment to read and feel each one. Let yourself, just for a few breaths, receive each one and imagine your life, imagine how you want to feel at the end of your days. Not to be morbid but to ignite purpose and connection with the deeper part of yourself who sees the truth of Amazing You. The part that leads you to reading books like this, that whispers (perhaps sometimes even screams) that your dreams are a calling from your truest self.

Regret 1: I wish I'd had the courage to live a life true to myself, not the life others expected of me

Regret 2: I wish I hadn't worked so hard

Regret 3: I wish I'd had the courage to express my feelings

Regret 4: I wish I'd stayed in touch with my friends

Regret 5: I wish I had let myself be happier

The simplicity of this wisdom is profound. It isn't coming from someone well-versed in selling from the stage, inspiring you to up-size your life. Those public presentations can be deeply moving and invigorate passion for action which is a wonderful thing. However, in a certain mindset, and depending on the presenter, it is easy to feel revved up in order to be sold to. These insights are coming from people sharing their deepest truths, at the end of the journey that we are all on. They've lived out the result of not knowing their Happiness Recipe or knowing it but not giving themselves the conditions they needed to be fully-expressed, thriving and satisfied with their lives.

There is a deeper part of you that is ready and willing to cultivate soul-deep happiness. You already have some insights into this from what activities give you Surface Happiness.

Journal invitation:

One by one, in any order you choose, spend at least five minutes with each of these top five regrets. Write down the whole sentence and allow any thoughts, feelings and energy to come up. I want you to imagine yourself as the wisest incarnation of you that you can imagine and allow your advice, wisdom and insights to flow from you onto the page. It doesn't need to be pretty. You're allowed to feel angry, trapped and unsure how you're meant to make any changes. It's important to let those limitations come up so that you can work through them. While they are quiet boundaries that keep you in dissatisfying situations, the light of day can shed no new wisdom.

You may feel that some don't apply to you, and that's OK too. Do your best to make them apply to your situation. For example, if you haven't done paid work for some time, what are you working hard at? If you feel that you do express your feelings, then look at the results of that and see if there is connection and relationship-deepening happening as a result. Are you expressing to the right people and is it helping?

You may finish earlier than five minutes. It's common to have a rush of words and then run out. Stay with it. Sometimes the real gems come after the stillness of mind.

If nothing comes to mind, write the questions down at the top of five separate pages and revisit the exercise later on. For some of us, the best time for this exercise would be straight after doing something off your Surface Happiness list, like leaving a yoga or meditation class, and feeling really connected to your own wisdom and guidance. If you love your job, then answer the questions after a great day at work. For others, that's when you feel the most content and least able to access advice for feeling better on account of already feeling great. For those people, you'll yield better insight when you're feeling disappointed or dissatisfied about something. That will be when you're most connected with what you want to change. You'll either find this easy or difficult, but either way, you are connecting with your care label and your own embodied wisdom, and that is always a good thing!

****

Cause and Effect

Our lives are an ongoing dance of cause and effect. Each moment, decision and action breeds the following. Each cause generates an effect and that effect becomes the cause for the following effect. The reason you are in the driver's seat of life is because you can actively choose 'causes'. I am breaking this down into such simple elements to highlight how much choice and therefore control you have over your outcomes. A well-used example of this is J.K Rowling's journey of publishing her first book in what became the Harry Potter series. When she submitted her manuscript the first time, it was rejected. What effect did this have on her? I'm imagining there was some sort of emotion, but she chose to submit it to another publisher. So often in life when we receive a hard "No", it generates the effect of stopping and giving up. Tapping into the beliefs you already had lurking inside you of 'not good enough' or other unhelpful self-framing. J.K Rowling was rejected over and over again and yet, "As of February 2018, the books have sold more than 500 million copies worldwide, making them the best-selling book series in history" [1]

So often people sit in blame, that they would be successful if only others believed in them enough and supported them enough. They would be wealthy if only they had that face, this opportunity, rich parents. The reality, as hard as it is to hear when you're in the thick of blaming the outside world, is that the only person who needs to believe in and support you, Is You. The level to which you are willing to put effort into yourself will determine the energy and effort you put

---

[1]   https://en.wikipedia.org/wiki/Harry_Potter

into finding the ways to move forward, even in the face of the repetitive hearing of "No".

We can sit in two basic positions in the way we think and feel about our lives and our options. I call them 'cause' and 'effect'. Whenever we get stuck in effect, we are giving the control of our lives to something or someone outside of us. We feel we are a victim of a person, people or circumstances outside of our control. We often surround ourselves with people who perpetuate this belief system. We feel deeply misunderstood and hurt when anyone disagrees that we are stuck and tries to point out options that we firmly believe are not options for someone like us.

When we step into 'cause' in our lives we see all the elements that are within our control, each and every moment of the day, and the power we have to stimulate improvements. What you invest your time into thinking, planning and ruminating over, what you say, what you eat and your portion sizes and how much time, effort and energy you put into your wholistic health, your relationships and the achievement of your goals is all totally within your control. I'm not suggesting that it's easy and effortless. What I am wanting to convey, hopefully in an inspiring and heartfelt way, is that your body, being and life experience is the end result of a whole lot of verbs. You can, right now, begin to change some of these 'doing words' in your life and this *will* create new effects.

I am also not suggesting that you use this tool of understanding 'cause' and 'effect' to quickly move out of uncomfortable situations without the learning they provide. For example, if you are in a romantic relationship and do not feel valued or respected an easy fix would be to ditch the relationship. Bam! No more problem. However, without any deeper investigation into the parts you played, you'll probably play out the exact same pattern in your next relationship, or, if you choose to give up on romantic relationships altogether, you'll most likely find the same relationship dynamics in your family, workplace or any other type of group you connect with. Now, you are well within your rights to keep moving towns, jobs, relationships and groups because everyone else is the problem. I'm not saying that they're not. You also have an amazing opportunity to practise new ways of relating in the relationships you're already in. By changing your part of the dance of interconnectedness, the other person can no longer do the exact same steps they're used to doing. In short, don't sit in 'effect' with other people's behaviour as your own is the other side of the dance.

Grieving is another place where I see a lot of people wanting to fast forward through the process. I understand the desire because it is so deeply painful to lose someone you love, under any circumstances. In the initial stages, which I call 'ground zero', we only use the 'cause' and 'effect' principle to be asking things like, "How can I nourish my body in this time?", "Who could call work for me?" Many well-meaning loved ones try to get grieving people into practical life organisation and 'getting on with it' far too early. I think of it a little bit like having major surgery. You don't want to be opened up and, as soon as you can stand, whiz out to the supermarket, or plan Christmas dinner. Slowly but surely, you take more steps and move further from home and take on more complex tasks, but if you're doing all of that in week one, then you're not recovering. Grieving is extremely personal. I could quite easily write another book called The Grieving Recipe, because it is a very individual process and, like happiness, requires a connected, open relationship with yourself that allows you to follow your needs and express them. Using the 'cause' and 'effect' principles to take care of your immediate safety, body nourishment and the support you need is what is important. It is later on in the process that we start getting into 'cause' with questions centred around the recalibration of moving 'on', into this new version of life that doesn't include the person or situation that is no longer with you.

Our next chapter is about Emotional Digestion and will talk in more detail about processing emotions and moving through them to the clarity on the other side.

I wish to thank the very talented James Tsakalos, NLP and Spiral Dynamics Trainer extraordinaire, for introducing me, back in 2011, to this very useful way of framing up communication in relationships. Most people that I have worked with talk about their relationships with others as if they are a noun. They talk about their relationship, their house, their car, like it's part of a list of solid things. 'Relationship' is the nominalisation of the verb, 'to relate'. What does it mean to you, when you describe a person as someone you can relate to? For me, it means that I can identify with them and understand them; we share a connection.

Over all my years of working in the depths of human experience, the vulnerable and powerful places of truest honesty, I have seen phenomenal transformations when two people choose to get out of their habitual patterns and change the way they interact. It usually starts with just one person doing it differently.

I will briefly describe the types of listening I have identified and I suggest you imagine, as you read each description, how this type of listening would affect the relationship.

<u>Listening to end the conversation:</u> You want to be polite but you also do not want to be in the conversation. So you wait for a break in the stream of sharing to excuse yourself or to provide a one-liner that shows you were listening and move on. In more active endings, you insult or bamboozle the person in whatever ways you've learned work to stop the interaction or turn the conversation over to another topic.

Listening to reply: You are listening and thinking about what to say when it's your turn to talk. Sometimes, not even waiting until it's your turn, just jumping in when the other person takes a breath.

Listening to defend yourself: You understand early on that the person is sharing something that may upset you. Perhaps it conflicts with your perception or opinion. You pick it up in their approach, their tone of voice or something else that makes you sure they're having a go at you. That they think and feel differently to you is upsetting and you're interpreting it as them saying that your feelings are wrong and they are right. You are now listening to defend yourself. This can mean butting in or waiting until the end to share your side but the whole time you are listening to make your points of answer more powerful, rather than trying to see things from their point of view.

Listening to argue: Some people really like listening to input another point of view, even if they have no strong feelings either way. They are listening for the weakness in an argument, to drop in there and point it out. This type of listening turns conversations into a debate, which is only fun if both people are into this style of communication and if both people get to actually make all their points rather than be overrun. For someone who finds sharing challenging, this is a very effective way to end their sharing. They would rather not be talking at all than have to fight to have an opinion or a feeling heard that differs from the other person.

Listening to understand: This is where you really put your focus into considering what the other person is telling you, or trying to tell you. We have often established poor communication patterns and things might be a bit of a stumble in the beginning (particularly if you've usually used some of those other kinds of listening). Listening in this way does not mean you have to agree and it doesn't mean that you may not be hurt by what is being shared. There is also no actual resolution without respecting that each person has their own unique perspective. In this listening, you will ask clarifying questions and step into the other person's shoes to try and see it from their point of view. You know that if you understand where the person's feelings are coming from, and in turn express your side of things, you have the best chance of stopping cycles of the same disagreements happening over and over again. You also know that this type of listening leads to deeper connections, trust and intimacy.

Listening is just one part of relating to the people you care about. Asking for them to listen to you in ways that cultivate understanding is another aspect. Imagine the changes in dynamics possible with even just this small shift.

Choosing how to listen is one of the many touch-points you have in causing new effects in all of your relationships. You also get to choose how you speak to other people and what freedoms you allow yourself in sharing your frustrations. You can choose to review your communication style. Is the way I'm sharing my thoughts and feelings inviting honest communication in return? Or am I being placated because communicating anything I disagree with creates a whole lot of judgement that I openly share. What would happen if I listened to understand? What could happen if I asked for this kind of listening in return? You can choose to share what you need to feel supported. You get to choose how you show your love. You can choose to share the ways you feel loved, what creates intimacy and connection and what creates the opposite.

How much energy and effort do you put in your relationships? Is it the kind of effort that is creating a feeling of supportive love for yourself and the other person? Are you paying attention to the feedback your effort creates and continuing to do something that is not actually creating anything positive? Do you resent this effort, even though it was never asked for? Are you focused on what you're not getting and not giving the time and attention to what you can give? Are you asking for what you need? Are you expressing yourself, your hopes and your frustrations in a respectful way that invites conversation rather than argument?

Are you in relationships where you're always thinking of others, making their lives better, easier? Focused on making sure other people feel loved and valued? Are you feeling valued by them? Have you shared this? If you feel afraid to share this, what support can you get to begin learning? If you feel that no-one really cares about how you feel, why are you putting all that effort into those connections? How bad does it have to get before you put yourself into the mix of people you care about enough to address their needs?

I have seen amazing turn-arounds in marriages where one or both partners had expressed to me that they were "done!". These transformations happen when both people choose that their relationship is worth the effort of listening to understand and working together on resolving the issues. I have also seen relationships where the most loving and respectful result is the end of the relationship. It can happen when, through really understanding each other, it becomes obvious that there really are irreconcilable differences that would always be an ongoing cause of passionate conflict due to huge differences in values, priorities and preferences. The wonderful part of this is that both people have worked through their relationship, valuing each other enough to really listen and understand, given each other the opportunities to really open up and learn about themselves. They both leave the relationship with an unforgettable upgrade in self-awareness and the elements important to them in future relationships. I have also seen huge transformations in the dynamics between siblings, parents and children, employer and employee when someone gets into 'cause' and names the disconnection.

Getting stuck in 'effect'

There are five decision patterns I've noticed in how and where people most commonly get stuck in effect.

1. This is just how it is, there's nothing I can do so I just have to live with it, make the most of it, 'suck it up', look on the bright side.

From all that you've already learned, you can see that embedded in this type of thinking is the notion that what's going on is not changeable. The person at 'effect' just has to dig deep and manage as best as they can. This is one of the types of stuckness where someone on the personal-development path will be using lots of Surface Happiness tools to keep their emotional head above water, but not addressing the core drain as it's immovable in their perception. I had the pleasure of spending some time with Lindsay Tighe after writing my first book. She is the author of, "Better Questions are the Answer" and has a transformative business based on this incredibly simple, highly effective premise. I couldn't agree with this idea more! When we assume that the core issue is unchangeable, we are only using the incredible resources of our own being, to ask questions about managing the stuck situation, rather than accessing our wisdom and generating options for the situation itself, releasing all the time and energy that goes into 'managing' it.

2. I'm not good enough, fit enough, supported enough, financed enough, smart enough etc.

This whole idea of 'not enoughness' is a self-perpetuating way of staying in 'effect' potentially for your whole life. There are lots of snazzy coaching questions that start to break this up, like: "Good enough compared to who?" The reality is that we are all works in progress. I guarantee you that there is someone throughout the history of the world, who wanted change in the area you want it, and who started with less than you do. We get to choose whether we focus on the countless rags to riches stories or the trust fund children who have seemingly endless financial resources through no effort of their own.

Take a moment and think of a skill you now have, that you weren't born with. There was a time when you were also 'not good enough' at that. With the intention of learning, time and practice, you now have that skill. If you get empowered and choose to improve one of those areas you feel 'not good enough' in, and keep at it, you *will* start to see changes. The reality is that you can put all that energy that used to go into 'not good enough' (in all its many forms) and use it to focus on what you're wanting to improve in. If you've mastered 'not good enough' then you can also master this new priority.

3. It's not my fault so I'm not going to be the one to fix it.

There are a myriad of ways to stay stuck in this. They don't listen to me so I'm not going to listen to them. They stopped talking to me so I'm not going to be the one that restarts things. They misinterpreted what I said, that's their problem, not mine. They believed lies about me so it's up to them to come and get my side of the story. I work for a family-owned company and family members are the only ones who get promoted, it's not my fault I'm still at an entry-level position. My family wasn't wealthy and couldn't pay for my education, it's not my fault that I have few job prospects. I could go on and on but I'm sure you see the pattern.

Now, all of these choices are legitimate options. We have free will and you get to choose. That said, if it's occupying your thoughts and draining your energy, you're not actually okay with it. If *you* are not okay with it, then *you* need to be the one to choose change. The change you choose may be some external support to move through your feelings, leaving the situation unfixed. Or, you may choose to directly assess the situation itself and get proactive about possible solutions.

4. Focusing all the energy on how and when it started, who started it and why.

There are a couple of ways to ask yourself, "Why?" One perpetuates victimhood and this will keep you at 'effect' indefinitely. The other is more about finding solutions through self-inquiry. "Why did this happen to me?" can become a pondering on the parts you played in the situation. This can then turn into ideas about how to do it differently in the future.

There are some types of support, both professional and within personal relationships, that quite literally keep people stuck in this place. Talking about how in the past they were hurt and let down and why it makes total sense that they now have no self-esteem. If you are wanting to take more control of your life and your circumstances, this kind of support is an empowering first step. The second step really needs to be focused on getting where you want to be, rather than settling for where you are and blaming it on other people, the past and things outside of your control. You have total control over what you focus on mentally. Even the busiest client I've ever had could make a little bit of time for setting a new goal and taking small actions regularly that moved them in that direction.

5. Using the notion that what's happening is a "first world problem" as a justification for staying mediocre; not making the most of opportunities because not everybody in the world has the same opportunities, therefore it's selfish, elitist or just wrong of you to want more than you already have.

Staying small serves no one! When we allow expansion into the best versions of ourselves, other people benefit. Think of how little money would be donated to charities if no one in the first world allowed themselves to thrive. A healthy way to move out of this stuckness is to focus on the ways you can contribute to those less fortunate than you.

The basic pattern to emerge out of effect and back into the driver's seat of your life is the same:

1) Have a desire for things to be different and improved.

2) Identify the core issue or issues.
    If you're not sure, start with one idea and work with that. In the process of following the rest of these steps, it will become clearer whether you're on the right track.

3) Ask yourself some questions like:
    What can I *do* about this?
    What other options might there be?
    Who else has had this issue and what have they done to overcome it?
    Can I adopt some of their strategies?

4) Try things. Make decisions. This is not an invitation to exhaust yourself on possibilities, it's about being willing trying new things. Even an attitude shift can create a tremendous opening for change. A change of just 1% will have you arriving at a different future years from now.

5) Notice how these new things feel. We have a whole chapter coming up on 'Embodiment' that will give you great tools for this step.

6) Respond to the feedback you experience. Human beings learn through trial and correction. As you notice the feedback, make some adjustments. Ask

yourself, what seems to be getting results and what isn't? What am I enjoying and what am I not? What parts will I continue on with? What elements need to change?

Life is precious. You are precious, powerful and truly magnificent. In the driver's seat of your life, you can travel the roads you were born to. It will take some of your time, energy and effort but remember you are already using those on the situations you want to change. So, I'm not asking for *extra* effort, just that you use some of your existing time, energy and effort on some *new* things. Take some of your everyday thinking time, to do some assessment on what's working for you and what's not. This is practical, embodied empowerment for an authentically lived life.

Emotional Digestion

I've heard some very interesting ideas, opinions and theories about emotions over the years. I've had numerous clients come to me with the goal to be less emotional and others wanting to access more emotionality. There are often harsh judgements flying around in these peoples' lives around their capacity for emotion, perhaps considered 'too much' or 'too sensitive' or 'emotionally stunted' and 'too harsh'. What we consider to be emotionally weak and what we think of as emotional strength will be based largely on our upbringing, socialisation and life experiences. For some, the peak of emotional strength is to have a devastating life experience and show little to no emotion; to have the fortitude to 'get on with it' and forge on. For others, the peak of emotional strength is to have a devastating life experience and to feel it, show it, share it with loved ones, learn from it and be able to move on. As I have said, human beings are not one-size-fits-all and this is just as true in how we move through life's ups and downs. Our next chapter moves into your individual care label, and your emotionality is part of this. There is no perfect level of emotional feeling and expressing that is right for everyone. That said, it is important for all of us, in our own, unique ways, to digest emotions rather than ignore them, fast-forward them or stay stuck in them.

Our bodies are living systems of ongoing processes. Living is a verb. We are designed to digest food *and* life experiences. There are really serious ramifications to our health and immune system functionality with ongoing diarrhoea, vomiting or constipation. The same is true with emotional processing, except we can learn to have such incredible control over our emotional digestion that we harm ourselves more than the original, emotional incident did. This is one of the many reasons why exploring your Happiness Recipe is so important. I invite you to think about emotional processing like the digestion of food.

Imagine a first-responder arriving at the scene of an accident. The ability to compartmentalise mind from body and feelings is incredibly important in this immediate situation. Decisions need to be made, getting people to safety and prioritisation of the injured. There isn't time to stop and feel any horror at loss of life. There isn't time to stop and sympathise, there is an internal prioritisation of where to put one's energy and focus. Heathy first responders have a system for doing this and then, once they're done with their part of the job, to process their own feelings. This kind of support is getting more attention now so that first responders can be emotionally, wholistically healthy enough to do their jobs well, in a sustainable way. In the most extreme cases of seeing strength as lack-of-emotionality, people can move through their lives like they are moving through an active battlefield. Not stopping to feel their own pain or anyone else's. This is only ever useful in the very limited short-term. In the longer term, it's like eating a huge piece of steak, not even really chewing it, pretending you weren't affected by it and having it sit in your gut for the rest of your life. No processing for me! What steak? It's over. Stop bringing up the past! This is what I imagine in my mind's eye when I hear, "Get over it!".

There are other ways to get stuck and avoid emotional digestion, and that is to stay in the parts of the process, prior to elimination. For some, they get stuck in the chewing. In the example of a relationship break up, this would mean staying for years in the thought space of analysis. Replaying conversations in your mind and holding space for mental-chess with all possible meanings, outcomes, how things went and how they could have gone differently in a multitude of scenarios. Sometimes, based on the body's innate knowing of emotional digestion, the process will move through into feelings and, due to our immense control, we can come right up out of there and back-track into mental investigations, other possible whys and wherefores and the same patterns of thought that have not (and will not) yield any new information for healing. Chewing is an important part of digestion but we need to move on and through to gain any nutrient value from the experience.

All three of these examples, the person in the battlefield, the first-responder and the chewing in analysis are ways of being emotionally constipated if you remain stuck in them.

For others, they get stuck in the feelings. They've chewed and have landed in an emotional state like sadness, fear, despondency, guilt, hurt, anger or resentment. Now obviously, there are recurring thoughts that go with this, too, but the energy of it is different. It's not really an analysis, there's usually been some sort of internal decision made, that becomes what is 'true' for the person. To use a break-up as an example: I just wasn't good enough. He/she was heartless; why do I keep choosing heartless partners? It was all my fault. It was all their fault! I'll always be alone and unlovable. They were obviously using me! They lied. There's something wrong with me. When stuck in this way, there's ongoing regurgitation of the same or similar feelings. What's 'true' remains and the feelings that perception creates remains, too. Over time, there might be a lightening of the emotion, due to other distractions, but when triggered into a memory of the initial, emotional incident, it has the exact same power to drag up those same feelings. The emotions are just as fresh and powerfully expressed in the body, even after many years.

I am going separate the two things happening in this state long term. The first is the their reaction to the actual, ground-zero event. Let's use the example of being made redundant at work. When a person is used to full-time work, particularly in a role that supported a healthy self-identity, there is a lot to miss when that major life-focus is off the menu, not by choice. It doesn't matter if they could see it coming or if it was a surprise, there will be an emotional reaction. Depending on the state of their finances, there can be other, stressful side-dishes that will need to be worked through. These initial stages of feeling and expression I call 'emotional gastro'. I came up with the term about ten years ago to help clients to understand that this emotion is not permanent. They haven't turned into a weeping wreck that will never function in the ways they want to again. The innate wisdom of their body is supporting them to release the charge of what's happening and not hold all that stress in their body. "Imagine", I say, "having gastro and thinking the 'right thing' is to hold it all in, don't express or release any of it . . . can you imagine the pressure on the body? There's going to be a blow-out somewhere else for sure!" Thinking of it like emotional gastro is a way of allowing your feelings to move out of you, that's what your body wants to relieve that pressure. Depending on the emotional situation, your time in emotional gastro is different. The loss of a job you didn't really like will be very different to the loss of a loved one you thought you had a lot more time with.

The second thing happening is how the event has been interpreted. We do take life personally because we are a person, interpreting life. When we touch a hot stove as a child, we usually learn 'don't touch hot stoves', not 'oh the stove didn't mean for me to take that personally'. It hurt you, it's personal, and it's an inside job to work through the feelings and decide what *you* would like to do with and about them. This may well be different to what someone else would feel is right to do in the same situation because, yes I've said this many times, we are individuals.

Now, once past ground zero, the parts that keep on hurting you are usually your interpretations and the 'truths' you decided as you begun to process your feelings. They hurt you in two ways. Firstly the actual belief hurts. If you decided that you live in a country where people over 50 years old aren't valued in workplaces, underpinning that belief is that the company you worked for stopped valuing you. Not because of your poor performance, you were doing great, but because of the year you were born. They've effectively said, you're no longer useful, you're not valid in the workplace, we don't care what you've contributed, you're past our used-by date. Those interpretations hurt, especially when you're someone who has lived your life with a strong work ethic and felt pride in what you have contributed in your workplace.

The second way this interpretation hurts is because of how it colours your potential future. This belief would most likely stop you from even applying for roles that would challenge and interest you. It may lead to you retiring early when you really wanted to keep on working because your work gave you so much (not just financially). It may stop you from really looking around at other people your age and what's happening for them. I have a client who was offered four jobs in her 60s over a two month period, because her passion for what she is doing is palpable and her dedication to results, obvious. And this role she was being hired for, was something she began after the family business was retired, career number three for her. The two of us laugh together that we will never retire because we both love what we do, and the life-changing impact we have, so, so much!

What we decide is true, during emotional processing really can keep us stuck in emotional gastro. The emotions may change from anger to despondency, but we are still stuck in feelings with no resolution.

"Every cloud has a silver lining"

Another common reaction to shocking and difficult

emotional situations is the desire to get 'over it' as soon as possible. Not staying too long in any of the steps, focused on the pursuit of feeling better at the expense of drawing worthwhile experience from the process. This is where a lot of Surface Happiness tools can be used effectively, but only to support the outer surface of your life circumstances. Again, to use partnership break up as the example, this would involve a lot of Surface Happiness tools and a premature arrival at 'I'm over it', 'I'm better now'. I worked with a client who came to me about eighteen months after his fiancé had unexpectedly ended their nine year relationship. He had responded to this devastating news by telling himself and everyone else that, while she broke it off, both of them were dissatisfied, it was mutual and he would have done it anyway at some point. He never asked her any clarifying questions, he didn't seek out any support and instead focused on his career and building fitness and muscle mass like never before. He came to me at the point where he'd decided to date again and was horrified by the emotions that were coming up. He was seeing it as 'going backwards', when in reality, he'd whizzed through the whole break up aftermath, generated premature 'healing' and was feeling those very important emotions for the first time.

This is the equivalent of emotional diarrhoea. You've eaten a meal and want to zoom through to the elimination as fast as possible. There's no stopping to chew or absorb. In these places, we are missing the silver linings; the life-nutrients present in these experiences.

It is an important step to move through the emotional gastro stage and sit with your interpretations. What have I made it all mean, about myself and about my life? Now, and for the future? Are these beliefs useful? Are they even true? This is all part of getting into 'cause' with where you are and the ways of moving forward, with less pain and more joy. The good news is that we can do this processing, even years afterward, and receive the powerful benefits.

Three benefits to healthy, emotional digestion

There are so many transformative life lessons that can be learned in the messy trough of life's down times. The kind of learning that instigates career changes and dramatic relationship improvements. New found connection to what truly matters to you and the bravery to communicate honestly about your values, priorities, needs, hopes and desires. Self-permission to act based on these new understandings about yourself and the life you wish to live. This is one of the positive outcomes from living a life that is mortal, and includes a whole smorgasboard of experiences from painful loss to joyous connection.

In feeling the lows and moving through them, you open to feeling the highs in a more fulfilling way, too. Emotional armour is non-descriminatory, it's going to numb your experience of the whole smorgasboard. I have worked with hundreds of people who have learned to block out painful feelings (with differing levels of success in this endeavour) but begin our work feeling that this hasn't impacted their ability to feel happiness, joy, connection and love. There is not one of them that would say the same now. Emotional communication, allowing your truest self to be known and loved, requires access to the whole of yourself. In the blocking of painful emotions, we sometimes stay in situations that are not serving us, not making the changes that listening to our feelings may engender. Whilst it may feel more empowering in the short term to 'soldier on', you are being robbed of the fullest expression of who you are. Emotionally digesting the pain of a relationship ending has the power to bring clarity and deeper connections to all of your other relationships.

The melting of this resistance to emotional digestion also enables easier access in day to day embodiment –listening to your body and being, and using this guidance to move through life. We have a whole chapter on this coming up but in the meantime, know that the emotional freedom and clarity that results from emotional digestion fosters an easier connection to this amazing resource.

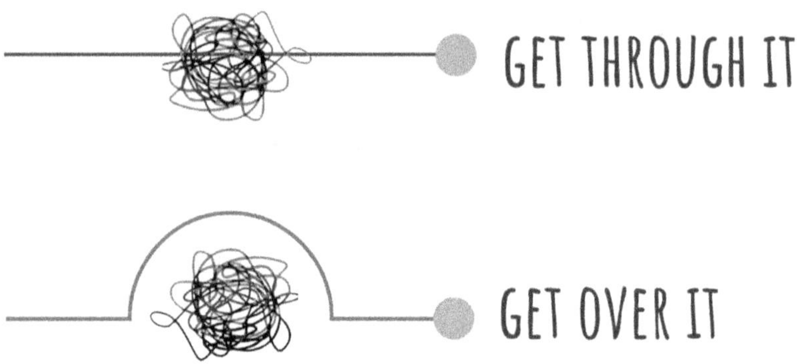

Being at that final circle is totally different, depending on the process you've been through. In the first, the memory has the power to destabilise you, over and over again. In the second, once through the experience, it is part of the rich tapestry of your life and the wisdom you have for yourself and others. There are three distinct elements to emotional digestion:

Original event - ground zero - and then:

- Chewing

- Feeling

- Knowing the lessons and what to move on from (elimination)

"A memory without the emotional charge is called wisdom"
Dr Joe Dispenza

The chewing and feeling parts of emotional digestion are important and not to be missed. Through these two parts of the process you are being preparing for what to keep from the experience and what to eliminate. Just like the digestion of food, our body takes the nutrients it can and discards what's not necessary. We can learn powerful truths about who we are, the strength we have and also who we want to be, by moving through painful experiences. Some of what we eliminate in the end, are things we've been told about ourselves that were never really true. Emotional digestion supports the evolution of ourselves and can really upgrade our lives when we allow it to. And, again just like our food digestion is aided by fibre, emotional digestion is assisted with loving and curious, self-enquiry.

Your Care Label

I invite you to take a deep breath into your curiosity. To begin this chapter with the understanding that there is nowhere to get to other than more self-knowing and self-acceptance. There's nowhere to get to because what you're looking for is not outside of you. It's been with you all along. There is no care label that is better than your own. We are not striving, in this moment, to have the best care label we can, the most exclusive or the simplest. We are aiming to gently set aside the ideas of who we're meant to be and land into who we truly are. And to learn what works for us, just the way we perfectly are, *right now*. We are settling into ourselves, to see our uniqueness with loving understanding and perhaps begin to see others through a different lens, too.

. DANDELIONS & ROSES .

I have seen such sharp and damaging criticism within relationships, from people only being able to see from their own perspectives. If these flowers were a certain kind of person, there would be a lot of dandelions bitching to each other and directly at the roses about being too sensitive, to picky, 'up themselves' or too posh. 'They think they're better than us because they smell lovely, well not *all* of you even smell that good!' And there would be a lot of roses commenting to each other and directly to the dandelions about being common as dirt, propagating anywhere and everywhere with no respect for planning or the hard work of others. And all the same colour, how drab! No scent, how boring. So low to the ground, they're beneath us!

It's strange isn't it, when they are both flowers, doing their best within their uniqueness, with the soil and circumstances they have available. If these flowers understood their care label and respected that differences and diversity actually makes our world a better place with more opportunities for all, we might hear different things. We might hear dandelions saying to each other, "Wow, they're so beautiful, so intricate and delicate. I love the aroma they bring to this garden and into homes all over the world. I really admire their protective thorns, too!" And roses saying, "Wow, I really honour the dandelions' strength and innate capacity to grow almost anywhere. I really appreciate their range! They remind me that nature is always making an effort and growing what it can, where it can. That gorgeous yellow is like a sunburst-reminder of nature's ingenuity. We appreciate a good prune, and they get a hell of a prune with the lawnmower quite regularly and keep on growing back. We both need sun and water. We actually have a lot in common, too, as we both add to nature's rainbow of beauty."

There is a wonderful freedom that we give ourselves when we stop judging our care label based on the care labels of others. When you give yourself permission to be you, you save a lot of energy trying to be what you're not. You also open up to having relationships where, "I love you" means I Love You. *You*! Who you are, not what you do for me, but the *you* that you've allowed me to see and know. Believe me, they feel very different.

Let's come back to the story of the ugly duckling, who was magnificent its entire life but measuring itself against a yard stick that never applied. It reminds me of the saying that everybody is a genius but if you judge a fish by its ability to climb a tree, it will live its whole life believing that it is stupid.

Experiencing the homecoming of self-acceptance doesn't mean that you're accepting that you'll always be exactly as you are. In fact, the only constant in nature is change. It means that you're ready to start from where you *actually* are because right here and right now is where all of your resources are. We can't start self-acceptance in 10 kilograms time, or in that promotion's time or when I'm healthier. In 'right now' you have a wellspring of potential. You are already amazing. You need start with your exact state of mind, body and circumstances. Not with the idea that they're substandard, but with the idea that you have now decided to have more authentic and lasting happiness in your life. From here, trial and correct your way into the improvements your whole being will benefit from.

Before we move into looking at some spectrums of self, I want to make a couple of things clear. Firstly, our care labels change through the ages and stages of our life. For example, some babies like a lot of cuddles and some are really happy having time on the floor and amusing themselves. I know; I've had two children and they were both very different in this department. As they've gotten older, it varies which one is the cuddliest. Right in this moment, it's the opposite of how they were as babies and, I imagine, it will continue to change over time. Secondly, our care labels change based on our circumstances. We discussed in the previous chapter the process of emotional digestion. When we are at ground zero with an emotional event or shift in circumstances, we may need a whole lot more or less of something than we do in regular, daily life.

If you're someone who really thrives with a predictable structure, you may be wondering what the use is of discovering a care label that changes anyway. Is it like buying a house, but it keeps moving on you and you never know where it is and how to find it? The answer is no. We are working through these concepts because they are part of your very own instructions for the care of you. Some of what we're about to work through you'll already know. When you're sick, you might need more sleep. When you're sad, you might want more company or less. It depends on your care label. The benefit of knowing yourself in this way is so that you can stop self-judgement and adjust your inputs and outputs as necessary, based on what is going on for you at any given time.

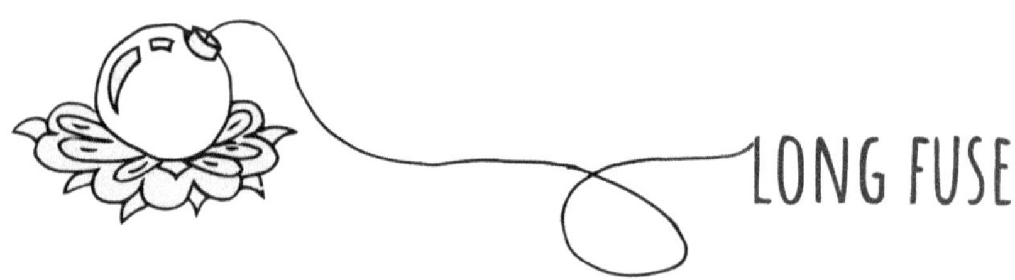

I am going to introduce you to the following terms: 'resourced', 'unresourced' and 'buffer'. When you are resourced, it means that you're feeling good; your cup is full. It is easy to take a breath and choose how to respond to what is going on and you have easy access to your wisdom. To use the analogy of a dynamite explosion, being resourced means you have a really long fuse, patience and ability to stay calm.

When you're unresourced, you're cup is empty. You are less resilient, and have less capacity for patience and kindness towards yourself and others. You're easily triggered into emotion and feel you have less control over your reactions. Using the dynamite analogy, your fuze is tiny, between event and kaboom!

Your buffer is how long it takes for you to blow your fuse, if crankiness and frustration is your go-to when unresourced. Or how long it takes for you to feel hopeless and defeated, if despondency is your unresourced go-to. For some, that unresourced state takes the form of sharp insight turned inwards like a blow torch of self-criticism; looking out at life, turning all achievements into pointless ashes, and glorifying failures. For others, being unresourced means "Don't ask me anything, don't talk to me, leave me alone", feeling overwhelmed by the basics, feeling like everything is collapsing.

I had a client once that used to refer to his buffer as his freeboard. It's a boating term that refers to how much space there is from the waterline to the upper deck. He struggled a lot with anger management before working with me as he was so out of alignment with his own nature in his life, and felt trapped in circumstances that he couldn't see the way out of. As we would sort through things, he would see all the ways he wasn't honouring himself or those around him, and understood why his fuse was so short. He learned what to communicate with his partner and how. What to shift and change and how. And the ways to free up more time for himself, to invest in solutions to his financial situation. After each session, he would describe that he felt more 'freeboard'. He was lighter in the waters of his life with so much more space between him and being filled to heaviness that felt like drowning.

It is important to get a sense of your buffer because, just like everything else, it differs for us all. So, access curiosity, rather than judgement and see the value of knowing these things for yourself. The more you're out of alignment with your Happiness Recipe, the less freeboard and buffer you have to navigate your life with. Just like we don't want to over-water and kill our plants, we also don't want to over-stress our buffer and get really depleted, out of self-ignorance.

Here are some spectrums to consider. They are not laid out in any order and there is no significance to what's ended up on the left or the right. They are a mixture of physical experiences, daily life activities, emotional and mental processes. It is by no means the total and comprehensive list of the human experience. That would be far too long and involved. This is a list purely to stimulate self-reflection. At some stages of your life you may have been quite different to how you are now. This doesn't mean you've evolved or de-evolved, it just means that you've changed. You may also be right up to the edge with one of these in your personal life, but want it to be different in your career. Just read through, notice what captures your attention, and any that have strong reactions for you, good or not. Not all of these are preferences. We all have different needs, based on our different bodies as well as different inspirations. Remember, no judgement of yourself or others, just open curiosity about marvellous diversity.

Where do you see yourself in these spectums?

BEING TRANSIENT	HAVING A HOME BASE
INTERNAL RECOGNITION OF SELF – ACTIVITY HAS ITS OWN REWARD	EXTERNAL RECOGNITION –THANKS, APPRECIATION, DEMONSTRATION THAT YOU ARE VALUED
ALWAYS CHALLENGING YOURSELF	STAYING WITH THE KNOWN
FULL HOUSE – LOTS OF PEOPLE INTERACTING TOGETHER	SPACIOUS HOUSE - LOTS OF ROOM FOR OWN PRIVACY
NOT A LOT OF TOUCH	A LOT OF MEANINGFUL TOUCH WITH PEOPLE & PETS
SHARING ALL EMOTIONS ABOUT EVERYTHING WITH MANY PEOPLE	SHARING ONLY THE MOST IMPORTANT EMOTIONS & ONLY WITH THOSE WHO ARE INVOLVED

STRUCTURE — FREEDOM

ALONE TIME — TIME WITH OTHERS

PLANNING — SPONTANEITY

SAVING — USING/SPENDING

SIMILARITY WITHIN WORK — — — — — — — — — — — — — VARIETY WITHIN WORK

LOVING INDOORS — — — — — — — — — — — — — — — — — LOVING OUTDOORS

BUSY LIFESTYLE, LOTS ON — — — — — — — — — — — — QUIET LIFESTYLE, LESS ON

PARTICIPATING — SPECTATING

WARM CLIMATE — — — — — — — — — — — — — — — — — — — COLD CLIMATE

HANDS-ON PHYSICAL WORK — — — — — — — — — — — — — CEREBRAL WORK

EXTERNAL PROCESSING OF — — — — — — — — — — — INTERNAL PROCESSING OF
EMOTION – TALK THROUGH   EMOTION – ALONE

LOTS OF ACTIVITY AND MOVEMENT — — — — — — — — — LOTS OF REST AND STILLNESS

QUIET — NOISE

EXPANSION, GROWTH — — — — — — — — — — — — — — CONDENSING, SIMPLIFYING

BALANCE - TIME FOR — — — — — — — — — — — — — FOCUS ON SINGLE PROJECT
MANY THINGS   UNTIL COMPLETION

STARTING — FINISHING

LEADING — FOLLOWING

TEAMWORK — INDEPENDENCE

ARRIVING EARLY, PLENTY OF — — — — — — — — — — — ARRIVING ON TIME, IN
TIME FOR ANY EVENTUALITY   FLOW WITH TIME, A BIT IS OKAY

EARLY MORNINGS — — — — — — — — — — — — — — — — — — — LATE NIGHTS

GROWING, EXPANDING,   ENJOYING WHERE YOU
STRIVING, FORGING FORWARD — — — — — — — — — — — ARE, CELEBRATING WHAT
TO BE EVEN BETTER IN   'IS' WITH NO CURRENT
WHAT YOU'RE PRIORITISING   PLANS FOR ANY CHANGES

LOTS OF SLEEP — — — — — — — — — — — — — — — — — — JUST ENOUGH SLEEP

TIME WITH PEOPLE, — — — — — — — — — — — — — — TIME WITH OTHERS, IN
TALKING AND SHARING   THEIR PRESENCE BUT QUIET

What elements of personal variety are issues in your life, that aren't on this list? Note it down and it's opposite, too.

Here is an example of care label wisdom at work: I worked with a client about five years ago who was really struggling with daily stress and extremely low quality of mind and mood. Bianca was working remotely on a community outreach project with severely disadvantaged people. She was in a small team; less than a handful of people. A friend referred her to me the year before because she was feeling a bit lost and listless in her work as a social worker in a large city. She had invested in all of her university study and work experience due to a strong and heartfelt desire to make a difference in the lives of others and had flat-lined in this role. There was a lot of bureaucratic red-tape to wade through and it was very challenging to feel powerless in making real and sustainable changes for the families she was supporting. She felt it was managing the situation, not changing it in the ways she could see were possible, for the families or their children. When she applied for this remote role, she was expecting to love it. Bianca imagined that this small team would be people like her, passionate about helping those who need it; not as charity but getting in there, within their communities with the support and resources needed. She came from a place of deep respect for the existing culture and circumstances and was so excited to be leaving her desk and making the difference she was craving.

When we had our session a couple of months into her new role, she was devastated about how she was feeling. She interpreted the despondency and stresses she felt as her not being cut out for this kind of work and was spiralling into thoughts like, "well, who I am then?", "I thought I was strong and I'm not coping at all!", "I don't want to go back to that old job . . . am I the kind of person who can really make a difference anywhere?". She thought the problem was her own capacity and personality and this was really crippling her previously-strong sense of self. She did describe a few issues she was having with the other staff, the differences in attitudes and the feelings of aloneness, but she wrote all of that off as elements she should have expected and been strong enough to deal with, which for her meant to be quiet about it and focus on the job. I am so glad that we had the sessions we did for her to come to understand her care label and her values!

The manager in her new role had a very different communication style to Bianca. Perhaps she was an internal processor of her emotions or perhaps she was shut off to them, but either way she was totally unwilling to discuss any challenging circumstances with my client. There was no support on offer for those really emotional days in this kind of job. There was a, "this is how it is, deal with it or leave" attitude and based on that, the team that was left (after a lot of staff turn-over) were all very similar. There was nowhere to go in the team for support, upwards or sidewards, and no growth or development available.

Bianca is a woman with very close, personal friendships. She has a core group of male and female friends and meaningful conversations with them, talking and sharing about life's ups and downs was a very important element in her life. In this remote role, there was no mobile phone reception. Once a week she was able to get to a town and have about an hour to herself, that she could use to connect with her loved ones. Add to this that she felt isolated with her workmates and shut down by her manager. For her, debriefing events with others helps her to move through and regroup for the next day. She was there with a passion to make a difference and with strong work ethic to be the best she could be in her role. She spent every night alone in her tent and got more and more miserable. Her beautiful heart, one of her greatest strengths, was being seen as a great weakness by others and this rubbed off on her. Her colleagues would talk about their roles like it was a plumbing project, rather than human beings in distress. There was no collective vision for improvement, it was more 'management'.

Her innate wisdom was giving her feedback that this situation was not sustainable. She is energised by social interaction, being around people and interacting with like-minded, like-hearted others. To feel enlivened by her work, she needed to see that her time and energy was making a positive difference. None of this was on offer and this is the reason she felt despondent.

I had the absolute pleasure of seeing Bianca this year, for support in a potentially tricky conversation she wanted to have with a family member. She was glowing! Radiantly healthy and so happy. The role she has been in for the last three years pulls together all that she intuitively knew she wanted. Her role is based out of a small city, with time also spent remotely. She has an excellent manager who leads the team from a place of appreciating the diversity they bring. The culture of her workplace is one of honour and respect, for the people they work with and for each other. She has made many life-long friends as so many of them share similar values and priorities. She has a home base in the city so that she's able to have friends and family come and stay on weekends or during her holidays.

She is now so familiar with her care label and so embodied, listening to her own wisdom, she said to me, "I'm loving this role, the people and my colleagues, but I'm feeling that I've probably got another year in this job before looking for the next challenge". The whisperings of, "there's something else to explore" were just beginning and she now knows not to wait until its screaming.

If you are someone who really thrives with challenging themselves, you will end up dissatisfied staying in the one job role with no dramatic changes or growth opportunities. If you are someone who really thrives on predictability, knowing your job and doing it to the best of your ability, changes can be quite destabilising. Knowing this about yourself will support you in choosing the right work and job roles for you.

I once dated a man who had a very fluid relationship with

time, in every area of his life. He would often be late for work, miss aeroplanes and be late to functions. We once arrived, after the bride, to a wedding. The experience of being his 'plus 1' for this wedding taught me a great deal. I was so stressed about running late that I probably produced enough adrenalin for every guest to successfully run for their lives once we finally arrived. I had never met a single person there, other than the person I was going with, but for me it was so disrespectful that I was horrified and embarrassed. For those of you who, like me, have a different relationship with time than he did, you may also be questioning his respect for the bride and groom to be. I could not understand how relaxed and comfortable he was with being late because he cared deeply for the couple getting married. He could not fathom how I could possibly be upset about it. For him, it was a total success that we made it in time to see all the vows exchanged. The parts that mattered to him, that were his demonstration of respect and care, were different. He had spent a lot of time researching to buy them a present that was a really fun and bonding experience they could all share together. He also explained to me that what really matters, to him and for them, is that we have the best night possible. That we stay until the end, that we dance and make an effort to get different groups of people connecting with each other and having a great time. That is what he put his energy into, that was the priority, and whether we snuck in after the bride was not important to him. Honestly, if we had have missed the entire ceremony, he would have happily watched the recording of it with them later. For him, the greatest disrespect would be been sitting in the corner and leaving early. For him, participation in the celebration, the party of togetherness afterwards, is the bit you can't re-do.

Had we ended up partnered for life, this would have been an area we needed to do some loving compromise with. Asking him to always do it my way would have been stressful for him, just as him wanting me to do it his way was stressful for me. Good relationships require curiosity and an openness to understanding each other's differences and the impact that our choices and behaviours have on them. From here, respectful compromises can be made, by and for each person. This man would never have held a job for an employer to whom punctuality was important. He did have some amazing career roles with people who wanted his fun-loving, people-engaging nature in their business and were willing to take those solid benefits and accept what came with it.

We can get suggestions and be inspired by those around us but the idea is to experiment with your own experiences. Any new ideas are not the answer or the way for you until they *feel* right for you. It is more feasible that you take an idea, try it, use the embodiment you'll be learning about in the next chapter to really feel how it's working for you, and then tweak it to suit. To make it yours.

A great way of seeing this in action is in the area of morning routines. Having a supportive routine in the morning can be a solid corner stone to the beginning of your day. There has been a lot of studies done and great books written on this topic. I was nineteen years old when I began my self-administered, personal-development journey. The first book I read was, "The Silva Mind Control Method" by Jose Silva. I loved the idea that the way you interpreted things, changed your feelings about them. I still use one of his spectrums in keeping my kitchen clean. He taught that you can look at dirty dishes and a messy kitchen focused on the mess the whole time you're getting it sorted. Or you can see the exact same kitchen and go into the cleaning imagining your beautifully clean, tidy and organised kitchen and how wonderful it feels to be in it. The thinking and resulting feelings are totally different. His book, released in 1977, was a game-changer for me as it was my first introduction to being able to choose an empowered perspective. These types of tools are usable for all of us, in all types of situations.

When it came to the books I've read about routines, I have not found the same useablility. Before becoming a mother, I was right into structures and daily routines. There were about fifteen things on my tick list for each morning before starting work. I used to tick them off each day, on a sheet I'd print for each week and give myself a percentage of success at the end of each week, as a way of keeping myself on-track and inspired for action. This commitment was a tool for Surface Happiness and also the Soul-Deep fulfilment of taking actions towards my dreams.

I caused myself a lot of stress, trying to find ways to still do all of this in the same way, when I became a mother. New born babies are not one-size-fits-all, just like the rest of us, and I didn't have one of those sleep-all-night-after-six-weeks babies. I caused myself a lot of totally unnecessary stress, trying to fit pre-mother routines into my new circumstances! My care label changed because my circumstances had changed. There was another, new and wonderful part of my life that my heart enjoyed prioritising.

Care labels change as we change, although there are usually some very common themes throughout our whole lives. Listening to your body's wisdom is so important because we need to pick up on the subtleties of buffer-shifting situations. There are very few things that will cut through a well-resourced person's buffer in one go. It's usually more of an accumulation. Let's use some examples to illustrate this.

Let's imagine you've agreed to help out with your child's school excursion to the museum. You spend the day with a large group of very excited and noisy eight year olds. The bus is alive with enthusiastic, white-noise and you need to be very alert all day, counting the children in your group (because the school would frown on any being left behind). You get home after this full day to a house-load of friends and family for a birthday party you are hosting. You spend the afternoon and evening, cooking, serving, chatting and cleaning. More people, noisily having fun, all around you. I have just described someone's perfect buffer-filling day and simultaneously described someone's buffer-eroding, day of depletion. It all depends on what makes *you* feel dynamically alive.

Our buffer is very naturally robust when we are living in situations matching our care labels and overall Happiness Recipe. Generally, having one thing go way off base, is totally absorbable. It's when they start to accumulate, that, with time and practice, you will start to really get those messages that it's buffer-filling time. For example, let's say you are someone who really craves time and space by yourself, loves spending a lot of time outdoors, working with your hands and creatively solving problems in a self-managed way. If you had a job for one week that was indoors, it would be okay. Perhaps not your best week, but there wouldn't be stress showing up in all the areas of your life. Let's consider however, if your job role was changed, due to new management. You are now working indoors, on a computer, with a huge team of very chatty people. They want a lot of small-talk and interaction through the day, not about work, just shooting the breeze about life and the world. Your new manager has very strict methods of how things will be done and has no interest in your creative ideas for improvement. In fact, he finds them insulting and insubordinate, so takes to a lot of micro-management and looking over your shoulder through each and every day. Can you imagine the accumulative effects of all of these changes, over the long term? Can you imagine the quality of your thinking? And what kinds of feelings those thoughts would be producing?

No amount of Surface Happiness is going to correct these fundamental mismatches. No amount of distraction, complaining or self-medication will either. Change only happens by getting into 'cause', learning to know your care label, noticing what resources you and what drains you, and taking *new* actions that will begin to shift what is not working for you. Soul-Deep Happiness and fulfilment is not attainable or sustainable, until we understand and accept our individuality and care about ourselves enough to start providing the conditions we need to thrive.

Embodiment

There are many schools of thought that teach mastery *over* the body. Almost like it's some inconvenient thing you need, but shouldn't pay that much attention to.

One of my early teachers of metaphysics and meditation gave these lessons, that personal evolution was rising *above* the messages of the body and connecting with blissful, spiritual (non-physical) knowing. And, in order to do this, you have to ignore your physical self. To this, I say that there are truths but also additions I would like to add. It is a lot easier to meditate when you're not in physical pain and we have more energy for personal evolution when we are nutritionally-nourished and rested. For both of these, you must at some points through your day, attend to your physical needs. I've also had personal trainers who instructed me to push through pain for just "ten more" of something; that the body was to be mastered for the previously-set goal. Again, there is wisdom in this, with additions necessary. Fast and hard rarely works with health and fitness goals unless you have absolutely flawless instruction, extraordinary embodied, self-awareness and *long*-term commitment. Hard and fast in the short-term creates so many more injuries than slow and steady. Hard and fast in weight loss, usually leads to most of the kilograms ending up back on, sometimes with a few extra coming, too. I have also hired life and business coaches who had the same philosophy. That once you set a goal, all resistance, stress or lack of motivation equates to some kind of self-sabotage. When it comes up, you need to push through, "go hard, or go home!". If you want to be successful you need to push, strive, hustle and get the stuff done, even if it feels uncomfortable or you are ignoring other parts of your life. Now, again, there is truth in here, but only if you are completely aware of what the discomfort is about and make an active choice to continue with the pace and goal you've set with full understanding. I cannot tell you how many clients I've worked with who have achieved miraculous work goals, only to reach them alone. Partners tend to leave if you don't ever stop to ask "How are *you*?" and are only focused on yourself and your goals. Your health tends to leave as well, if you don't give your body the tools and ingredients it needs.

Caring for our physical selves and listening to our embodied wisdom is of great importance so as to have a pain-free, energised body with which to enjoy your successes!

Our bodies get a bad rap in many religions, too. This notion that the needs of the body are basic and *beneath* the wisdom of the human heart and mind. That sensual pleasure is self-indulgent or sinful. That being a sexual being is only acceptable in a tiny, narrow way (decided long ago by someone other than yourself) and the rest is distasteful and disgusting. Glorifying abstinence over experience. Praising innocence over wisdom. Learning from childhood that the basic needs of your body are wrong creates a lot of guilt and shame. Families with the idea that children even knowing the name of their body parts is 'dirty' create adults without the freedom to feel wonderful about their whole, physical self. It's acceptable to know that you have a knee and a chin, even seen as clever for children to know the correct names for things, but to know that you have a vagina or penis is outrageous and they're 'not ready' for it. Imagine if children were taught that urinating was wrong, that they should never, ever pee or they were going to be in flames for all eternity. Can you imagine how much pain and suffering would occur? That peeing would continue to happen because it's a basic human need and so is touch, love and connection. Babies need skin-to-skin touch to help them thrive and grow. Happy hormones are released when we hug for more than 20 seconds. Touch and connection with our bodies is actually really important. Your care label will determine how much of this works best for you in your life right now, but the need is there for all of us in some capacity.

I invite you to think of yourself as a powerful fusion of mind, body, heart and soulful essence. In my experience, when we incorporate the body into wholistic life, we create more enjoyable and sustainable circumstances. The reality is that whatever experience we are having in life, we need our bodies to have the experience. It is through our amazing bodies that we are able to see, touch, hear, smell, taste and sense our lives and the world around us. So, regardless of whatever opinions you have about your body's size, shape and features, it's an amazing vehicle that makes your life possible.

Your body is the result of millions of years of evolution and two hundred thousand years of human evolution. There's a whole lot of information we carry, even before we add the heart, mind and soul to the alliance of You. I think of body's cells as the most loyal and hard-working staff one could ever have. They are always striving for the balance that we need for health. They work hard, every moment of every day, from birth to death, always doing their best, regardless of how well they are treated, loyal to the end and passing on what they've learned to their offspring. When we can give our bodies what they need, when we can make the job of survival easier by resourcing our vehicle, we free up so much energy for healthy, happy vitality. Our bodies are designed to be giving us the moment by moment feedback that they're giving, to support us in making that possible.

Our diet for health is not just what we put in our mouths. It is the entirety of what we consume. Along with food and drink, your diet consists of the air you breathe and the people you choose to interact with; what you watch, read and the information you ingest. One of the most important elements, that underlies so much of previous, are the thoughts you're thinking. Your existing program of beliefs and what captures your conscious attention, moment to moment.

You are in your own company every single day. You are the only person that you will spend every waking (and sleeping) moment with for your entire life. The quality of your relationship with yourself has an incalculable effect on your state of mind, health and quality of life. I have a whole workshop that addresses this called "Practical Self Love". I was inspired by all the people that seemed to know they were meant to love and care for themselves but had no idea how to actually *do* that. The beautiful Louise Hay introduced many of us to mirror work, the essence of which is looking at yourself in the mirror and saying positive affirmations. For some, mirror work created positive miracles. For many, they would embark on this activity only to stop and get distracted by feeling their face or body was ugly and enter a whole, well-practiced string of negative commentary. "Practical Self Love" teaches you, functionally, to care for yourself in the way you care for others and I highly recommend it. Self-love and self-esteem provide the right fuel for making healthy choices in the whole of your diet, to set respectful boundaries in your relationships and to create time and space for your priorities. In this chapter, we will be focusing on your internal dialog and the ways of connecting with and receiving the wisdom of your body. Both are tremendous contributors to your sustainable happiness.

Internal dialog – the inner conversations with yourself

The way you are thinking about yourself and about your life inside the privacy of your own mind has an immense impact.

I think all of you reading this book would understand that a parent who puts their child down with messages like "why can't you be more like ____, you're such a disappointment!", or who focuses on what they see as deficiencies, will not be supporting their child to feel valued, to grow into trusting their judgement and have confidence in themselves as they move out into adulthood. When you talk to yourself in the same or similar ways, focusing on what you think you're bad at, comparing yourself to others in a self-deprecating way, giving attention to your failures, you are effectively parenting yourself to feel smaller and less capable than you are. You are talking yourself out of the confidence that would be yours, if you framed up your situation differently. You *do* have choice and control over your well-practiced thought patterns. It may not feel that way if you have had decades of certainty that you are somehow, inherently 'less than' others but it is true.

In modern culture, even our own personal development has been seduced into the push and strive for "bigger, better, faster, more!" Anyone who's read "The Lorax" by Dr Seuss knows this isn't sustainable and yet the number of expensive workshops promising the end of all your negativity and self-sabotage in just one weekend, continue to grow. It is absolutely possible to experience single moments of profound self-awareness that forever change your perspective on your life and what is possible. I have had this experience myself, many times. Sometimes in workshops, sometimes with a coach or mentor, sometimes in meditation or while doing something mundane like making the bed. The fine print for these experiences having lasting value is what you do with them *afterwards*.

I once posted on my Facebook business page a picture that read, "Until you change your thinking, you will always recycle your experiences." Someone commented that deep meditation can achieve this, too, and I agree, in part. It is still a mental decision to prioritise meditation. To make it a daily practise. To decide on learning and continuing to practice. It is also in the realm of your internal thinking to decide to act on any guidance or new understanding you receive. For example, in meditation you may realise that the share house you live in, is no longer the right place for you. It is still in the realm of your mind that you make the decision to look for somewhere new to live, to share your decision with your housemates and how you'll share it. You may want to express your feelings, you may want to share in a way that doesn't blame or hurt others unnecessarily. Both sharing your decision and moving house will take some thinking and planning. My point is that a flash of insight or coming home to a new, deeper understanding then moves into the region of your thinking and the resulting actions chosen. It takes practice to apply your authentic truth into the world outside of you.

Your Internal Radio Stations

I invite you to think of your mind chatter and intentional contemplation as radio stations. For the purpose of this introduction, we will focus on the main two: The supportive and encouraging, Positive FM and the self-deprecating, demeaning, Negative FM. You may find that you have a few more, like one that does total distraction, fantasy and imagining of wondrous events that you have no intention of ever turning into goals. It's great to have a station like this, in the same way that people like to watch movies and be entertained. It is only something that needs to be worked on if your balance is off. Returning to your care label, if health and fitness is important to you, or socialising with friends, and you're sitting alone for weeks invested mostly in Fantasy Distraction FM, then you're going to feel it in the longer term. Just like listening to the actual radio, there are lots of options and as it's only you, with no one else's preferences to consider, who can choose to change the station.

Negative FM

Your negative radio station holds all the files of negative experiences and self-perceptions, and also the thoughts that take you out of 'cause' and back into effect. I call these joining thoughts. They begin the seduction back to Negative FM and it's important to know the joining thoughts you have that slip the inner radio dial for you.

Negative thought examples:

I am so stressed; life is stressful; I suck at this; things will never get better;
Remember when _____________ - cue instant feelings of embarrassment, shame; It's all ___________'s fault that I'm like this, damn them!; whenever I relax, just a little bit, things always go to hell; I am so unlucky; I'm ugly, fat, useless; I'm a loser; what's the point of any of it; the world is doomed; people are evil; no one even cares anymore.

Joining thought examples, bringing you back into effect:

Things haven't really worked out for you in the past, why will this be any different?
You're trying so hard and yet it's so easy for those other people, who already have _____. What would ______ think if they knew what you were trying to do?
You're so tired, you're always so tired, why are you even trying?
Remember when _______ - cue feelings of disappointments, times you've let yourself down or been let down by others, dreams not realised (that you gave up on).

Positive FM

Your positive internal dialog holds your actual positive

thoughts and records of positive experiences and all the joining thoughts that bridge the gap between being at 'effect' and moving into 'cause'.

Positive thought examples:

What a beautiful day; I'm so grateful for the time I have right now to be reading this book; I am so grateful for my body, that can receive this information and use it to be feeling better; I like that I'm the kind of person who wants to be happier.

<u>Joining thought examples, bringing you back into cause:</u>

I get better at what I practice, this is really important to me so I'm going to keep on practising and noticing the parts that are getting easier and encouraging myself along the way. If I was able to do _______, then I can do this as well. Okay, I'm not liking this feeling/experience, what can I do about it? What could I change? What would start to make a difference? Who do I know who's made changes like these? I can ask them. Who could I hire for personalised support with this? Are there any books, podcasts, websites on this exact thing that I can learn from?

Remember when _______ - cue feelings of successful completion or accomplishment, goals reached or a positive situation that still brings a smile to your heart and mind.

When you've listened to your own, negative self-talk for a long time, the radio dial is used to sliding back there. You will need to catch it and dial back to where you want to be. This will take practice and effort. It is this practice of listening to your positive and encouraging radio station, and tuning back to it if you get a bit seduced by the dark side, that lays down the new neural pathways. The only way for this type of thinking to become your well-practiced normal is . . . to practice.

It is the same process as learning to speak a new language. You may have a desire to speak Spanish, an inner knowing that this will be wonderful and open up new life experiences. The desire and the knowing do not make you fluent in Spanish. It is accessing lessons and practicing, as often as you can, that will take your mind from one that can think and say, "Buenas noches", the greeting of Good evening, and request a tortilla at your local Mexican restaurant into a mind that can think in, and therefore speak in, fluent Spanish. It takes time, energy, effort and repetitive practice to become fluent in a new language. If you have been a 'glass half empty' person, in most types of situations, for most of your life, expect change to require effort and, use your new radio station to appreciate all the changes along the way. For someone with a positive radio station around learning new things, as they gain more Spanish dialog, they get more excited. The focus isn't on how much there is to learn, it's on how far they've come. When they can have a brief, simple conversation with someone in Spanish, it's a joyous occasion. The same can be true for you as you notice yourself responding differently than you have before. If you experience what feels like a set-back and instead of saying, "I'm so crap at this" you are able to say, "I'm learning this and as I practice I'm getting better and better" then you are making great progress. What my clients repeatedly report is that they learn to celebrate how quickly they notice the slide back into old, negative thinking patterns. They may have begun our work with their belief that they are a negative, guilty and unmotivated person. When I hear them say, "Oh, I had a bad day last Wednesday, spent half the day in that old thinking and feeling awful" I get so excited. In my mind, what was "normal" has become a state of being that gets their attention for half a day and embedded in that sharing is that, at some point last Wednesday, they got themselves out of that focus and on to thinking and feeling better. This is momentous! It's life-changing, because eventually it will be a rough hour and, with enough practice, you can feel the shift in your body and being when you first start entertaining self-deprecation. This is how it is done, just like learning a new language, with a building of dialog and skills to use the new framework in more and more situations.

Journal invitation - Name your radio stations:

This will be deeply personal to you. The more you personalise the process, the more light-hearted you can be when you catch yourself listening to those viscously mean, angry and stress-enhancing thought-tunes. Or the old, droning, heavy, energy-vampire of a radio host, playing the depressing thought-tunes. For your negative radio station, use words or a phrase that you often say when listening to those kinds of thoughts about yourself. I've had students who call this radio station things like, "Life Sucks FM", "Stupid Idiot FM" and "Why Bother FM". I have had students name their positive radio stations with things like, "Things Are Getting Better FM", "I Can Do This FM" and "Loving Life FM". For those with a more established positive mental framework, it may be more of a reminder, like "Life's Actually Wonderful FM" or "I'm Amazing FM". You can always change your radio stations later on, as you change your radio host and the thought-tunes you naturally play most of the time. The important thing is to meet yourself where you're at. What do you think would have happened if "the little engine that could" was listening to his radio station that chanted, "you know you can't, you're tired, you're so small, look at all the bigger trains that can do it easily, life is not meant to be this hard, what are you trying to prove, stop and rest, you deserve it, they're all laughing at you"? We all know what happened as a result of chanting, "I think I can! I think I can! I think I can!" and continuing to take that action towards the goal.

Name your radio stations so that you can easily recognise them and engage your ability to choose what you listen to. This is such an important part of your daily diet for health!

Underneath the radio station name, write the common thought-tracks that get played and any joining thoughts that get you back to listening. Do this for Positive FM and Negative FM.

****

Just like radio stations have a specific frequency that you need to be tuned into, in order to receive the message, your internal dialog has a frequency, too. What you invest in pondering, considering and repetitively thinking about will fuel your stagnation or your positive growth. Isn't it wonderful that you can start actively participating in this? You can get into 'cause' with your own, private, internal world and make changes that no one else will even know about. Prepare yourself for the changes that will start to happen in the rest of your life, as your new normal becomes more hopeful and self-affirming.

I want to draw your attention to two things that typically happen, in the beginning, when we are starting to exercise our power in shifting internal radio stations. Firstly, our minds are used to hearing the whole track of a certain line of thinking. When we first notice that we are replaying an upsetting situation, our body wants to get to the bit where we are telling that person off, or when we reach the bitter end of how alone we feel. We don't yet have the neural pathways for stopping, mid thought. It's like a train stopping where there is no station. At first, the passengers don't realise that they can open the doors and climb down to the ground, they're waiting for the platform and the doors to open the way they usually do. It's okay and totally normal for it to feel a bit weird, stopping that well-worn thought in a new place. Your mind might urge you to just continue until the known station, but the more you switch tracks and realise that you can, you're laying down new neural pathways and it gets easier and easier. The second mind-trap of the beginner, is when they realise they're listening to Negative FM, and use this awareness to stay in Negative FM to berate themselves. They land in, "see this isn't really working, it's too hard, I'm so broken and damaged that I can't make these changes like other people can, it would be easier if only _________ wasn't happening, it's not my fault I can't change". Everyone does this in their own, unique way so I can't capture everyone's specific internal dialog. Just watch for this negative commentary about the fact that you're listening to Negative FM. You are laying down new tracks of noticing and then learning to shift instantly. Once they're laid, this gets easier and easier.

I invite you to think of it this way: your mind is like a chainsaw. In the hands of someone who has practiced enough to know what they're doing, a chainsaw is a marvellous tool. You can use it to cut down a tree, large enough to keep you warm for a whole winter. In the hands of someone unaware of its power, who is using the tool haphazardly, a chainsaw can cut you so badly you bleed out on the ground – game over. Now, in the process of learning to use a chainsaw, if you noticed that you'd made leg-contact, instead of wood-contact, would you keep on going? Or would you immediately change tracks?

Listening, in an ongoing way, to Negative FM quite literally bleeds out your energy and vitality for life. I'm not suggesting becoming a mindless, positivity robot – there is no Soul-Deep Happiness available there, because you're missing the essence of you. Negative and positive experiences, and everything in between, are part of the smorgasboard of life. Noticing the negative and feeling our feelings, helps us to cultivate a more satisfying future that's more in alignment with who we are. The only thing that's wrong about Negative FM is staying there, and believing the mind-tracks that are playing, and not getting into 'cause' to make the experience useful.

Receiving the wisdom of your body

How you think generates how you feel. How you feel, and the resulting chemicals your body produces, directly impacts how easily your body is able to heal, maintain and repair itself. Even a committed atheist, western medicine practitioner knows that stress is damaging for the human body. You will know, from your own life experience, how different thoughts effect your tension-levels or joy-levels. How you feel when the phone rings in the middle of the night is going to depend on how you interpret it; whether a loved one is hospitalised in intensive care or due to give birth. That is your thinking in action. When you call a friend and they haven't yet called you back, it's the meaning you apply that will create the feelings. Amusement at their absent mindedness, fear for them that something may be wrong or deep hurt that you care about them more than they do about you. I'm not saying that these feelings are incorrect, but making the point that your thoughts have created the feelings rather than the person who has not called you. When we blame external circumstances for our feelings we engender powerlessness. When we claim our power, and love ourselves enough to cultivate the conditions we need to thrive, it changes our perceptions and our relationships. We can learn to communicate with people more honestly, share our perceptions and feelings, and relationships become clearer. It may be clear that the relationship has really unhealthy foundations and needs to change or be moved on from. It also may be that the relationship is even more wonderful that you realised.

Thinking and feeling are an inseparable loop of physiological experience. That is why it makes so much sense to include the body and its wisdom in our life-goals. This trusting of our body's wisdom has many names. Some call it your intuition, some call it your gut-feelings, for others it's just the knowing, without knowing how you know, or getting a sense of the 'vibe' of things. Let's look at a few of the more obvious feedback signals, before moving on to the subtler signals of congruency your body is always sharing.

Have you ever been in an emotional situation and had that ball in your throat like someone is strangling you or you have a ball of tension behind your Adam's apple (also known as laryngeal prominence)? There are two types of situations where this is common. Firstly, in an emotional situation where your body and being has tears being unshed. Perhaps because allowing emotion to show is challenging for you or perhaps because you are waiting before allowing it to come through and out. I know when I attempted to read the eulogy for my Nana's funeral thirteen years ago, that throat tension was like a fist. In that instance, I was unable to go on, I unconsciously surrendered to the tears, they flowed and my sister came to the rescue and read until I could compose myself. I have tears flowing down my cheeks now as I remember that sadness. This is the power of thinking and feeling. What we think about, remember, imagine and focus on is having a physiological impact right now, even when thinking about something that hasn't happened (and may never happen) or something that happened long ago. It was a long time ago that I last shed tears about the loss of my Nana. I usually talk of her easily and happy memories make me smile and laugh, focused on the love and not the loss, but in that moment, writing of that memory, I connected deeply for a moment with my experience and the memory of it that will always be there.

Unexpressed anger is another way we experience this ball of throat-strain. Perhaps there is something happening, wildly outside of your value-set, that you feel unable to stop or express your opinion about. This might happen in a work situation, where decisions are handed down from upper management and there is no option, in the moment, to express the strong and instant emotional reaction you're having. It can also happen in families with a strong culture of obedience, rather than open invitation for all to share their thoughts and feelings. In these situations, your entire being is bursting with the desire to scream or shout, to name the injustice or to make it right. It is being held in, the energy you would use for this action being contained, and this causes the tightness.

I worked with a client over a period of years, Linda, who was originally referred to me by a chiropractor. Linda was seeing the chiropractor due to ongoing neck and back pain. Linda, now in her 50s, had grown up in a large family of sons and had been taught that men in families make decisions. She was socialised to have no voice of her own. She experienced abuse, but it never occurred to her to tell anyone. She learned not to share anything of a personal nature with anyone. She married early, as a way of leaving her abuser, and it felt so wonderful to be loved, but she never thought about herself, her needs or her own wants and desires. For her, being loving was doing whatever her husband wanted and the reward was being loved in return. They had three children and they, too, learned never to consider her as she had, quite literally, never asked to be considered. She didn't share opinions or ideas, she gave to and supported other people's ideas and opinions. When they conflicted with her own feelings, she squashed that down, she never said "No", and just gave some more. The vertebrae in her neck and the back of her chest were always moving out of alignment. In chiropractic terms, this is called a subluxation, and it refers to a slight dislocation of the vertebrae. When these bones are not in the correct position, it can create pressure or irritate the nerves, which can cause them to malfunction or interfere with the signals travelling over those nerves. Your nervous system controls and coordinates all the functions of your body and when signals are interfered with it impacts the body's ability to function at the height of its innate abilities. These ongoing subluxations were a problem. The chiropractor would do his realignment work and by the next week, they'd be out again, hence the referral to me. She was exercising regularly but not losing the weight she wanted to.

She was getting regular massages but not ever releasing the tension she carried. Not releasing the stress from her past nor the pressure she was continuing to add to every day but not sharing anything but 'yes' and 'everything is fine'.

Over our time together, she learned her Happiness Recipe. She learned how to consider herself, as one of her loved ones, when she was responding to those around her. Slowly, but surely, situation by situation and relationship by relationship, she learned how to communicate her feelings and then her hopes. She trained people to consider her, rather than assuming her answer would always be "Yes". Every single one of her relationships changed for the better. Now she's thriving, looks a decade younger, has changed her career and daily priorities to include herself in the mix. And, just in case you're wondering, she still sees a chiropractor, once a month for maintenance, but her entire body is totally pain free.

Some of the obvious messages from your body are sensations like stress, dread, despondency and fear. Stress is so normalised now. There are even courses you can take on 'stress management' that are not focused on resolving the ongoing stressful situation, but rather tools, often Surface Happiness tools, to cope with it. Writing this book and sharing as loudly as I can, the tools I've seen change lives, is one of the ways I'm releasing what would otherwise be a ball in my throat about the absurdity of this kind of reaction. If you've broken your leg, the pain is your body signalling that it has new needs. Re-alignment, rest and support while it heals itself. It wouldn't make any sense to keep doing all your daily activities and just take better and stronger pain killers as your body's feedback gets louder and louder. Treating mental and emotional stress and pain this way is why breakdowns happen. This is how we end up in burned-out depletion. No ongoing, stress signals from your body should be ignored or 'managed'. It's feedback that something needs to change! We also need to notice the other kinds of messages. The ones that feel peaceful, relaxing, exciting, hopeful or uplifting.

Later in this book, we will explore your values and priorities. I want to mention here that sometimes we make choices that cause short-term sensations of discomfort for long-term life gains. To once again use the language learning analogy, if you chose to fast-track your learning, you might go on a holiday and immerse yourself in a place where your new language is the only communication option. You may initially feel a bit foolish or embarrassed, especially if you are someone who usually feels confidently competent and are unused to being the new and inexperienced kid on the block. If we always run from this kind of discomfort, we will always remain in our current zone of competency. When we want to make changes, we have to actually make changes and they won't all automatically feel wonderful. The more resilience you can build, the better. This is *not* resilience to stay in dishonouring situations, it's resilience to stay on the learning path to an outcome you have chosen that *does* honour you.

As I've already said, your body is communicating with you every moment of every day. These larger signals are pretty difficult to miss but we still have the option of choosing to ignore them. We really do have free will to manage ourselves. You now also have the option to really listen and begin to work with your body's wisdom as the priceless asset that it is. It is giving you moment to moment feedback, specifically tailored for you. It holds the records of everything you've ever seen, heard, smelt, felt, tasted and sensed for your entire life. It's got more information about you then any other person could possibly ever have. That is why external opinions are great to listen to and be inspired by, but they are not the way forward for you until *you* try them out and see how they work *for you*. Someone else's fingerprint isn't going to unlock your phone. Someone else's passion for adding strawberries to every dessert to improve them won't work for me because, for whatever reason, I don't like strawberries. This is why you need to get to know your beautiful self and your body is the perfect guide!

Congruency signals

We will move now into the more subtle world of recognising your own congruence. By getting to know your body and its signals, you can use its lifetime of experience to support making decisions that are supportive of your ongoing, authentic happiness and health.

There are three basic congruency positions. Yes, no and the place in-between where you're not sure. Just like everything else, you'll get better and better at recognising your signals with practice.

Yes

The affirmative position has a huge range. Everything from

"Hell yes! Let me at it right this second!" to "Yes, that's true". As we are all different, there are no universal situations that are an instant "yes" for everyone. For all of us, the "Hell yes!" parts of life will be different, too.

It is important for the following experience to get the most of your attention possible. I want you to really tune into your body and feel its reactions. We will start with some basics. Tune in and feel how your body responds when you say the following, filling in your exact truth in the gaps:

My name is ___________________

I currently live in ___________________

Right now, I am ___________________ (it may be sitting, lying down or out driving or walking if you're listening to the audio book)

So, it might be something like this: My name is Julie. I currently live in Austin, Texas. Right now, I am sitting on my loungeroom couch.

Do it for yourself and pay close attention. What happens in your body?

It may be so subtle that it takes more practice to really feel, so let's move on to what will most likely be a stronger sensation. I want you to think of something that, for you, would be an instant "Hell yes!" It may be winning a pile of tax-free money. It might be an all-expenses paid holiday to the destination of your choice, the negotiation of leave from work thrown into the mix on offer. It might be the opportunity to meet and share time with someone, alive in the world right now, who you really respect and admire but don't actually know. It might be that moment on your wedding day, marrying the person you adore and feel adored by, when you are asked your part of the vows, the part you need to say "Yes" to, in order to be married.

Just ask yourself the question: What would I say "Yes!" to, right now, no questions asked? Something that every fibre of your being will consent to with unbridled agreeance. A situation where there is no coulds, shoulds or would-be-better-ifs. Now, halt all other activities, pay attention to your body and all of its senses and ask yourself, "Do you want to do _______ now?"

What happens in your body?

Think of someone that you would love to hug and be hugged by. Imagine them opening up their arms to invite you into that embrace. What happens in your body?

Common signals of congruency are things like:

- A sense of warmth or spreading of warmth somewhere in the body

- A feeling of openness or expansiveness, either energetically or a physical opening of the body, movement of shoulders back, heart-space more open

- Relaxation in the core and/or base of your body

- A sense or feeling of relaxation, a letting go; a comforting sinking into peace

- A flurry of excitement, upward movement of energy like happy butterflies

- An internal tone of voice that's similar to your conversational "Yes, how wonderful!"

- A widening of your eyes

- The feeling of blooming openness, energy moving upwards and opening

In the practising of noticing our congruency signals, it can be necessary to equate ourselves with the opposite, to really feel the differences.

<u>No</u>

Complete these sentences with something completely untrue. Your name will be nothing like your actual name, as will where you're living and what you're doing.

My name is _________________
I currently live in ___________________

Right now, I am _________________

So, it might be something like this: My name is Jackson. I currently live in Hobart, Tasmania. Right now, I'm on the treadmill at the gym.

Do it for yourself and pay close attention. What happens in your body?

As with the gentle, "Yes, that's true, but it's not really that exciting", the incongruent signals can be easier to notice with the more extreme examples. So, right now, think about something that, for you, would be an instant, very strong and certain, "No!" It may be a job offer for a job type that's abhorrent to you. It may be the offer to eat something that you wouldn't want to touch with a barge pole, let alone put in your mouth. Perhaps it is imagining a nightmare-style scenario where you find yourself at a wedding, being asked "Do you take this person?" and it's an ex of yours that you broke up with years ago because the relationship was awful and they never showered (I'm just adding the sense of smell to enhance our "No" experience). Think of what would be a certain, irrevocable "No" for you. Now, halt all other activities, pay attention to your body and all of its senses and ask yourself, "Do you want to do ______ now?"

What happens in your body?

Think of someone that you would not want to hug or be hugged by. Imagine that embrace coming towards you . . . What happens in your body?

Common signals of incongruence are things like:

- A tightening around your gut, heart, chest, throat or face

- A sense of backing away, either energetically or as a physical movement

- A sinking, shrinking or contracting feeling, either energetically or with your shoulders moving slightly inwards, contracting of your core muscles or in the base of your body, a slight lifting of the pelvic floor

- A shuddering or vibration

- An internal tone of voice that sounds similar to your own voice making harsh commentary or issuing a warning

- A tensing of your eyes

<u>Maybe, not sure, more information required</u>

The in-between place of 'not sure' is somewhere we have all been, and will be again. Our wise bodies, who are aware of all of our history and know us so well, know we need more information in order to make a choice.

Consider these examples:

You are offered your dream job role without any information about the specifics. Depending on your circumstances, it may need to be within a certain travelling distance or come with a specific minimum salary to meet the commitments or current quality of life you wish to keep meeting. The flexibility of managing your own schedule or working some days from home may be important, so you'll need to know if that's available before being able to say 'Yes' or 'No'. Perhaps none of those things matter for you, but you will need to know who the current CEO is, because the culture of the organisation being in alignment with your values is even more important than the role itself. You will want to ensure that you're using your talents to contribute to what you believe in, and not enhancing practices that make the world worse off, in your opinion.

We will be moving into your values in the next chapter, but for now, imagine yourself in this situation. You're being offered a job with no practical details. You know you would love the role but you need to ask questions and find out more.

Feel what 'not sure, I need more information' feels like for you. What happens in your body?

Let's feel into 'more information required' again. You are talking with a person you have just met. Perhaps you are single, and are wondering if you'd like to go out with them. Perhaps you're an employer, and you are interviewing them for a job vacancy you want to fill. Perhaps you have just moved house and are talking with your neighbour for the first time, with a question in your mind as to whether they may end up being a friend (or someone you'll avoid).

What happens in your body?

Try this one: you have a need for a new car and you have some not-negotiable requirements. For example, you may be really tall and not comfortably fit into every car. You may be quite short and need for there to be adjustable seat and steering wheel options. You may have three young children and need to fit three car seats in the back. Perhaps the style of the car has changed a lot over the years, so you'll need to know what year it was released so you have a sense of the body shape of the vehicle. You may want the car to be new and not second hand. You may want the paintwork to be perfect, but not really care about the carpet. You may have a tight budget or want the car to symbolise your success, so the price will be really important. We all have our preferences and that is OK. So, imagine yourself in this situation and someone tells you, "I have a car you'll like" with no other details in their opening statement. It might be a perfect fit for your needs, or it might not be. You need to know more, right?

What happens in your body?

We'll do one more. You're standing beside a pool, in your swimming-gear ready to go, and want to go in the water. You have no idea what temperature the water is. If it's take-your-breath-away freezing, you know you won't want to go in. If it's hot like a spa, you'll be a bit hesitant but might try it for a while. If it's just right, you're an instant, "Yes! Here I come" and will jump right in. So, you're standing there, ready to get in the water, but you need to know more. You don't have all the information you need to be a clear "Yes" or "No".

What happens in your body?

Common signals of "Not sure, I need to know more" are things like:

- An uplifted feeling, like an expectant energy, ready to move, when ready. Like when you've decided to stand up, from a seated position and your body brings the energy for the movement before you have actually moved your muscles.

- A sense of upward movement

- A hesitancy, like small backwards and forwards motion, either energetically or sometimes expressed physically with the body or hands

- A scrunching of the face. I, quite literally, call it the 'maybe' face.

- An "aaaaahhh maybe" internal tone of voice; "ohhhh, not sure". There is often a bit of a drawn-out tone, higher pitched than regular tone of talking voice.

Journal invitation:

Go through these examples and make some notes. Create your own yes, no and not sure scenarios. Play them out and note how your body responds to each of the three.

How can you imagine using this information in your day to day life?

****

Congruency over time

What I have offered you here is a simple and powerful beginning to understanding the signals your body is providing you with. The real-time feedback around how aligned you are with your authentic self. As you get more and more familiar with trusting this, you will get more sophisticated in the application. One of the distinctions that is really important right at the beginning of your practice is the inclusion of time. How something feels in the immediate, is different to how it is going to feel when completed. For example, you may be told by a health professional that you need a blood test. Perhaps you've had really low energy, and you're tired more than makes sense. They want to check your vitamin and mineral levels. You may have had a negative experience with a test like this in the past, or have a fear of needles, so the instant congruency reaction to the test itself, shows up like a 'No'. The question then is around the ramifications of having the test results. Do you want to resolve this tiredness and have more energy for life? If that's a 'Yes', then you have a solution-focused direction. Perhaps then you ask yourself if there is another way to determine whether you have a deficiency that is causing the symptoms. If there is, then you get to ask yourself more clarifying questions. What are those other methods? What kind of time will they take? You then check your congruency around those options. In the end, you may decide that the test is the fastest way to get resolution, and therefore it becomes a 'Yes', not to the needle itself, but to your own choice of moving forward that way, into an experience you'd rather not have, but to get a result you've chosen you want *more* than the desire to avoid the needle. You may also choose to follow one of the other options. Perhaps, based on your research or your understanding, they will provide the fastest results or be the most nourishing. The fantastic thing about being an adult, aware of your own Happiness Recipe and willing to follow it, is that *You Get To Choose*. You get to choose whether you get a second or third medical opinion. You get to choose what activities you experiment with on your self-led, authenticity-driven journey through life.

Here is another example of congruency in the moment, compared with over time. If you are nervous with aeroplane travel, and need to get somewhere in a hurry, your initial congruency feelings about getting on that plane may be a 'No'. If you really feel into the event you want to get to, and that is a strong 'Yes' for you, it is possible to move into the experience, connected with the broader congruency around why you are going, rather than how you're going to get there.

Health and fitness is another excellent example of congruency over time. If you are unfit, the idea of getting off the couch and going for a hilly walk would feel like a 'No' in the immediate moment. The only people who are really loving every minute of exercise, are the people who are *already* fit. If your body is used to being mostly sedentary, it will usually feel uncomfortable with the beginnings of your new goal. Like those thought train-tracks we talked about last chapter, it is used to things being a certain way. If you are doing a bit of a cleanse with your diet, you may feel a yearning for sugary treats that feel like a 'Yes', but this is different to the long-term 'Yes' of feeling radiantly healthy and energised for life. This is why having congruent purpose in our actions is really important.

The next chapter is about your values. This will really support your usage of congruency over time, rather than in the moment. You will have more inspiration and self-motivation for values-aligned goals! I wanted to raise it here so that you have it in your awareness. The skills you are acquiring through this chapter will also help you to identify your core values. Our bodies do not lie to us in this regard, that is why it is so valuable to have your entire, wholistic self, take part in the unveiling of You.

Values

Your values are your significant beliefs, guiding principles, ethics and codes of conduct. Core values are what you hold in high esteem and attach the most importance to. They will include standards of behaviour along with what you respect, admire and cherish. Values often operate in the background of life, contributing to strong reactions and emotions, both pleasant and unpleasant. What you truly value being present in your life experiences, is fundamental in living with authentic and sustainable happiness.

I've heard many politicians over the years saying that they share my "family values". Knowing what I know about the human mind and how we interpret sentences like this, helps me to see that this proclamation means absolutely nothing. It's a 'need more information' signal for me. Some families value obedience and submission over co-operation and inclusivity. Some well-intentioned families can lovingly guide, suggest and even force their children onto paths that fit their own perceived societal values, without consideration for their child's individuality. In some families, one person makes all the decisions and in some, everyone runs their own lives and they come together, once adult, as equals. In some families, smacking a 'naughty' child is being a good parent, committed to raising a law-abiding and considerate child into adulthood. In others, gently explaining right from wrong to a child and conversationally working through a 'naughty' choice is what creates that law-abiding and considerate adult. There are no 'family values' that are universal, just as there are no 'families' that are. What is interesting to note, and will help you in uncovering what *you* think is most useful and important, is that we all have parenting values, whether we are parents or not. The parenting that you judge lacking, is highlighting to you the values-installation you feel is missing. The parenting you admire share some core values with your own. This is why it is so important to get to know yourself, ideally with an open curiosity, like a young child, free to explore in a garden. It is perfectly fine to take on the values of those around us, to see what we admire and aim to emulate that. Where the tools you are learning today will come in useful, is if you are not truly and deeply happy with where you are and where the road you're on is leading.

Knowing what you value will support you in making decisions that are right for you, in every area of your life. Values guide your purpose, in your work, your finances, your relationships and community. They will help you find your purpose, support and guide your goals and life direction. Understanding your values will help you make clearer decisions. Recognising them will bring clarity to any dissatisfaction in your circumstances. Certainty around values can also assist you in clearing out unnecessary life-clutter. And, if building your confidence and self-esteem is important to you, then this part of the book will be crucial. True confidence comes from being confident in who you actually are. Self-respect comes from respecting this true and authentic You. Putting time, energy and effort into being what you are not, is like the magnificent swan, trying to be a duck. Perhaps the swan could have put more effort into learning their ways and have found a place that was less unwelcoming, but it would never have been its fullest expression and neither will you, while you're trying to fit in and flourish out of alignment with your truth.

It is possible to work or live, side by side, with people who have differing values. In workplaces, communities and society as a whole, we really thrive with diversity. We need great leaders and inspired people working towards outcomes they value. We need inventors and creative thinkers and the people who buy and trial all the new things that come out. Their early-adoption leads to the modifications that make the 'new' thing more usable for us all. We also need the people who use the same tool for thirty years because it does its job perfectly and doesn't need to be replaced, regardless of what's happened in the marketplace. We need people in our communities that value different kinds of knowledge. Personally, I value learning about how to best support people into their most authentic self-expression, from a place of total self-acceptance and watching their lives come alive with this energy. I hire people to take care of what I don't want to invest time and energy into, like how to create new websites or service my own car. Thank goodness there are other people who thrive on getting that happening for me and others! It means we don't have to be everything to everyone, we don't have to try to know everything. Can you imagine how exhausting that would be? And how dissatisfying, if you value being able to do things well? One of the common causes of stress that I see is when people are trying to do too many things with the excellence of a master, who only had to spend their life on one of those things.

. PLATES ON STICKS .

If your life occasionally feels like the circus act of plates on sticks and you're tense from the fear that you'll drop plates any time now (or judging yourself for the plates that you just couldn't keep up and spinning) then you are trying to do too much! Clarity with your values will smooth the path to feeling so much better about yourself and about your life. Some of the plates you put down will be elements of life you truly value, but will need to come into practice a little bit later or in a way that takes less of your time. To paraphrase Marianne Williamson, we can have it all, just not all at once. This is why in our next chapter, we will springboard from your values and into your priorities.

We are going to move through three separate exercises to support you in uncovering your values.

Journal Invitation - Values elicitation exercise one:

1) Identifying values:

   Think of three separate and different events in your life where you experienced a peak of personal fulfilment, flow of alignment, deep happiness and/ or contentment. It may have been a moment in time or a period of time. It may have been a single and specific element that caused the feelings or it may have been a synergy of circumstances that brought it all together for you. Take yourself back into each of these memories, separately, and take notice of what was happening for you. Who was there or not there? Where were you? What was going on for you, inside of yourself and in your external environment and circumstances? Take note of all the elements that you believe contributed to this fulfilment and wellbeing and also anything that grabs your attention, whether it makes sense to you or not. This exercise will begin to highlight what is most important to you.

2) Looking for supressed values:

   Now, take yourself into three separate and different moments in your life where you have felt deeply unhappy, angry, frustrated, hopeless or blocked.

Take yourself back into each of these memories, separately, and take notice of what was happening for you. Who was there or not there? Where were you? What was going on for you, inside of yourself and in your external environment and circumstances?

Take note of all the elements that you believe contributed to this lack of fulfilment and flow and also anything that grabs your attention, whether it makes sense to you or not. This exercise will begin to highlight the values-alignment that was missing in those times.

3) Looking at your values around codes of conduct:

What behaviours and choices do you most admire in others?

What behaviours and choices do you resent, despise or get most upset about?

****

Journal Invitation - Values elicitation exercise two:

Here are a list of common values. Ask yourself the following questions, while looking through this list:

What feel like the essential elements of my life?

What do I really wish I had more of?

What do I resent missing out on?

Beyond my basic needs, what brings the greatest sense of fulfilment to my life?

What is, or would you like to be, your primary way of being?

What supports you inner self, your essence?

Now view the list below an make a note of the ones that really stand out as important to you and another kind of note next to the ones of some importance. Add whatever comes to mind, while doing exercise 1, if it is not already included in this list.

ACCOMPLISHMENT	COURTESY	INNER-STRENGTH	RESON/LOGIC
ACCURACY	CREATIVITY	INTEGRITY	RESPECT
ADAPTABILITY	DECISIVENESS	DECISIVENESS	REST/LEISURE
ADVENTURE	DEPENDABILITY	JOY	RESULTS (RATHER THAN PROCESS)
ALTRUISM	DIGNITY	JUSTICE	RISK
ANIMAL RIGHTS	DRIVE	KINDNESS	SAFETY
ASSERTIVENESS	EMOTIONAL INTELLIGENCE	KNOWLEDGE	SECURITY
AWARENESS	EMPATHY	LEADERSHIP	SELF-DISCIPLINE
BEAUTY	ENCOURAGEMENT	LEARNING	SELFLESSNESS
BEING LAWFUL	ENDURANCE	LIFE EXPERIENCES	SENSITIVITY
BOLDNESS	ENVIRONMENTALISM	LOVE	SERVICE
BRAVERY	EQUALITY	LOYALTY	SEXUALITY/SEXUAL CONNECTION
CALM	ESCAPISM	MASTERY	SHARING
CHALLENGE	EXCELLENCE	NATURE	SIGNIFICANCE
CHARITY	FAIRNESS	NURTURING	SOLITUDE
CLEANLINES	FAMILY	OPEN-MINDEDNESS	SPIRITUALITY
COLLABORATION	FINANCIAL SECURUTY	ORDER	STATUS
COMFORT	FREEDOM	OUTER-STRENGTH	STEADFASTNESS
COMMITMENT	FULFILMENT	PASSION	STIMULATION
COMMON-SENSE	FUN	PATIENCE	STRUCTURE
COMMUNICATION	GRACE	PATRIOTISM	SUPPORT
COMMUNITY	GROWTH/DEVELOPMENT	PEACE	SUSTAINABILITY
COMPASSION	HARMONY	PERSERVERANCE	SYNERGY
COMPETANCE	HEALTH	PLAY	TRANSPARENCY
CONNECTION	HOME	PLEASURE	TRUST
CONSISTENCY	HONESTY	POWER	TRUTH
CONTENTMENT	HONOUR	PROCESS (RATHER THAN RESULT)	UNITY
CONTRIBUTING	HUMILITY	PRODUCTIVENESS	VITALITY
CONTROL	INDEPENDENCE	QUALITY	WINNING
COURAGE	INDIVIDUALITY	RECOGNITION	WISDOM
	INGENUITY	RELIABILITY	WORKING HARD

Which of your marked items showed up in the first exercise? Can you see some themes emerging?

****

Journal Invitation - Values elicitation exercise number 3:

These three questions will help you to see where you are now, in relation to living in alignment with your values. It requires a level of honesty with yourself that can be quite confronting.

1) What do you spend your time actually doing?

   Take yourself through the last week or two and the twenty-four hours in your days. How much time are you working? If your work is varied, how many hours on each element of your job? For example, do you spend some of your day in meetings, some quoting, some doing the 'do' of your role? How many snippets or chunks of time do you spend on the various screens in your life? Be specific. How much time watching television, reading fiction or non-fiction. How many hours are you contributing or receiving from your family, cleaning, organising yourself or others? How much time is spent with friends or other people, on the phone or in person? How much time are you spending contributing or receiving in other ways?

   If you are currently blissfully happy, then you will be spending a lot of time in alignment with your values. If there are frustrations, then this will help you to see them more clearly.

2) What do you spend your money on?

Go through your banking statements for the last few months.What are you investing in? Where is your money going? If you have shared bank accounts, which transactions are yours and which ones are from other card holders? I want you to explore what you are prioritising in your spending.

If you are currently blissfully happy, then you will be spending a lot of your funds in ways that are alignment with your values. If there are frustrations, then this will help you to see them more clearly.

Now, take some time and have a look at the cumulative information from these three exercises. What are the common themes? What comes up in them all? If you have a huge list of values, we need to condense them down a little. This final questioning exercise will support you in your clarity.

3) What would you cancel over what?

This requires you to dig deep into your new embodiment skills and get very honest with yourself. Given two options, which would you prefer to do? Now, if you feel into the options and you know that, in practical day to day life, you would choose one over the other, but then resent it . . . you know you're out of alignment somewhere. As an example, in families with more than one adult, who cancels their plans to be with a sick child? When the option is go to work or be with my unwell child, what is being chosen? What is being prioritised? And how does that feel? When you're saving up for something but an opportunity comes along that you don't want to miss, what gets prioritised? The money saving or the opportunity? And how does that feel in the short and long term?

***

When I have gone through this in live workshops and in one-on-one work with clients, I regularly see two common outcomes. Firstly, a thorough and useful understanding of the person's current issues and emotional reactions. Secondly, a way forward into setting some new standards and priorities. We can't make plans to get more aligned with our truth until we see what's out of line. We will now move into your priorities and make use of all this fabulous work you've done, investing time and energy into yourself. Your future, happier self is already thanking you!

Priorities

"We either make ourselves happy or miserable. The amount of work is the same."

- Carlos Castaneda

You are now equipped with a lot of empowered insight and understanding. If you have given yourself time and space for the exercises in this book, you have the essential ingredients for your happiness recipe to explore. It is now time to make implementation an important part of your active, daily choices. The key word here is: explore. To take what you've learned and investigate. Try things out. See how they feel for you. Not for anyone else, but for unique and already-wonderful You.

From your third values elicitation exercise in the previous chapter, you will have undeniable clarity around what elements of your life are getting your time, financial resources, energy and focus. Now that you have shed light on what you truly value, let's ask these two question of ourselves:

How much of my regular, daily life, reflects my values?

How much of my time and energy am I spending on what really matters to me?

Having reached this point in the book, you may be pondering a whole-life overhaul. You might be thinking of major shifts like changing careers, the way you parent or your diet and lifestyle choices. You may have decided to transform your internal dialog or take on painting classes because you've realised that you really need a creative outlet. You might want to learn ways of feeling more honestly with yourself and sharing more honestly with others. Here's the thing, if we decide on making a whole lot of significant changes at once, we are much more likely to end up playing some Negative FM. Perhaps, "You're failing again", to the tune of "It's raining again"? Making changes to what is your daily practice of 'regular life' can take a lot of readjusting until it becomes your 'normal'. It can be tedious and frustrating and may need your undivided commitment and focus to get through the little humps where we can lose sight of the progress made. If you choose *one* change as your priority, you're much more likely to put in the repetitive actions that make significant change possible. When I'm working with a client who wants to change the way they relate to others, we usually choose one relationship to begin with. As we work through new ways to have conversations with this person, and they begin to see changes, those new skills do feed out into other relationships. If we began with the goal to change every relationship all at once, it could feel overwhelming and there may be hesitancy in beginning. It would also be a bit like that plates-on-sticks picture, and potentially feel more like managing a whole lot of moving pieces, rather than a central, empowering shift in confidently sharing who you are, and relating more honestly, to connect more deeply.

Have you seen or heard about the philosophy lecturer that first introduced what is now called the "Pickle Jar Theory"?

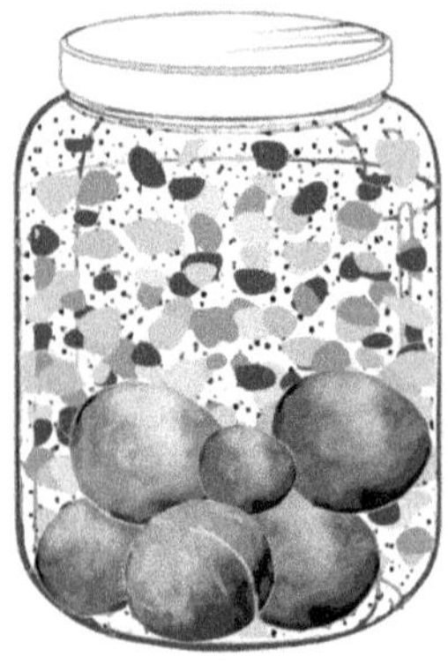

This clever, visual representation is part of what I had been doing with clients for years. The jar of our life just is not big enough for sixteen, equally important top priorities. It is also impossible to fit in the most important rocks, if our life-jar is filled first with sand and pebbles. We are living our practical life in a three-dimensional world that has twenty-four hours in each day. I am not, and will not, ever suggest to people that they just do more and push more to succeed more, without looking at what can be stopped or done differently. Burning out serves no one!

Rocks – Large and important tasks that represent your core values and top priorities

Pebbles – Tasks with commonplace importance

Sand – Smaller and less important tasks

This is why it is so important to be at 'cause' in your life. To intentionally create the space for your most important rocks, *before* you put in the pebbles and the rest fills with the sand of day-to-day living. Otherwise, the time just never arrives for those more significant tasks or events; the 'one day' dreams of your life that could be started now, if you made the time. This is especially true if they are of a long-term nature, like learning a new language, getting a university degree or an extended, overseas adventure. There is no 'one day' that magically arrives, without you giving yourself permission to make it a rock that's going in your jar.

The wonderful and freeing part of looking at your time and energy allocation now, is that you have permission for your priorities to reflect You, and to explore the right balance for you. There are many life coaches that preach pumping more and more into your day; like copying the morning routine of some super successful guru and getting amped up for Up-Sizing your life. I've found that there are very few people who operate congruently in this way. And, if you're going to try out a part of someone else's life, please take note of what is happening in the rest of it. If you've been up and out of bed to your children four times in the night and still need to get up, get everyone organised for the day and head to work yourself, your body will probably, quite sensibly, want to prioritise sleep over writing in your journal. Most very successful people have support that you may, as yet, not have. I know that for me, getting business-action, "must-do-if-I'm-really-serious-about-success" lists from a married man with a supportive house-wife, when I was a single mother with two children, was impossible to follow congruently. I had, and still have, very strong congruency signals around how many hours a week I work. I'm really clear on my values and priorities that way and have learned to personalise and individualise ideas and advice from *anyone* outside of myself. No one is an exact replica of my personality, values, priorities and circumstances, so what works for them is obviously going to need some trial and correction to be absorbed into my life in a way that's optimal. If we accept that from the get-go, it releases any 'why doesn't it work like that for me' judgment and invites, 'Oh, how interesting, I wonder what parts of that might enhance my life' curiosity. Remember, you are not broken, you don't need fixing. You simply needed more knowing and prioritising of *your* ingredients for healthy and sustainable happiness.

Let's look at your life-jar and pull together all that you've been investigating and examining so far.

Journal Invitation:

What are your most enjoyable surface happiness activities?

What is on your care label for that soul-deep fulfilment?

If you don't have a clear idea of that as yet, what would you like to prioritise the exploration of?

What came to the surface in your values elicitation exercises? What have you realised needs to be included and what needs to be eliminated or postponed? What needs to be increased or decreased?

What would you like to prioritise?

****

All of these insights can form a list of elements that you would like to include in your life experience. In many cases, this list may feel longer than the hours you have available. Later in this chapter we will explore ways to free up your time. Before we move into that, you will need to identify the core elements that you wish to prioritise. Some of these will be ways of being that you will consciously choose to incorporate into your activities. For example, if kindness has revealed itself as a core value, you can continue doing what you do and bring kindness into all of your interactions. It doesn't take extra resource allocation to be kind to others. Bringing kindness into your relationship with yourself, doesn't take extra time, it will just take a reallocation of your mental focus and internal dialog; a changing of your inner- radio station. A firm commitment to stop-in-its-tracks the mind-chatter train that's heading down to the well-worn train tacks of "I'm an idiot" FM, or whatever you named your negative station. All of this is happening in the privacy of your own mind, regardless of what you are currently doing with the rest of your body. Just like learning anything new, you will get better and better at inner and outer kindness with the practice you choose to prioritise. Other elements will require a conscious decision to reallocate your time with a shift in structure and planning. For example, balance may have come up for you as a core element you really need to thrive. If your life is currently way out of whack, and one life area is draining the bulk of your resources, some review, reshuffling and reframing will be necessary.

Both the inner changes, like what you mentally give energy to, and the outer changes, like creating more life-balance, need to be prioritised. Imagine the pressure you would create if you decide on five new, internal focuses. You would be all over the place! Having just the one will make it easier to shift out of old radio stations and into the chosen, prioritised, internal environment you value. Here are a couple of examples:

In late 2001, I decided to learn Greek. Learning and development has been a core value of mine for a really long time. Learning a new language was a new type of brain-food that I adored. Very strong "Hell yes!" congruency signals, before I had even heard of embodiment or congruency. For twelve months, this became an internal and external priority. I listened to Greek lessons or the local Greek radio station every time I was in the car alone. I was not yet a parent and had a very long drive to work each day, and to the college I was attending, so I got a lot of really fun learning done on route. I also incorporated this learning into other quiet life activities like cooking or when I was out walking. I had a full-time job and was also studying but with this being a priority, I weaved it into many other parts of my life. The only structure change required was the two-hour lesson with a teacher once a week. The rest was using the time I already had, in a new way.

Fast forwarding to 2009, I committed myself to a period where cultivating gratitude was a priority. I was a single parent, raising two children and running my home, business and personal life. My schedule was full! Gratitude became something I gave mental focus to, each and every day, often in creative ways. I wanted to train my mind to focus on all that I had, to feel wonderful about my life, and the opportunities I had to craft my future. In that time my practical circumstances were difficult and very challenging. The core values of providing financially and emotionally for myself and my children *and* being the present, conscious parent I wanted to be, were in competition for my time. My one year old daughter was very unwell and I was trying so many things to find solutions to support her. I was only having very-interrupted sleep each night. It was extremely rare to have more than a couple of hours in a row. I would have to change my clothes many times a day due to baby vomit and let's not even start on the bed linen. One person, with so much love for my two children and passion for my work, with only one lot of 24 hours each day. Honing my mind to gratitude was an amazing practice and honestly, the best fuel for my ongoing energy and vitality. I'm not suggesting it was easy, nor am I going to lie to you and say that there weren't, at times, feelings of desperation or tears of exhaustion. I just committed to myself, not to drown in those feelings but to use my intelligence, creative thinking and imagination to focus on solutions, and gratitude for the resources I *did* have in my life. It was in this time, digging deep for positive reframing, that I felt gratitude for elements of my life I'd never before considered. At the end of 2009 I bought my first home and felt indescribable gratitude for all the women who had come before me, making my reality possible. I was an unmarried, single mother and yet I had never experienced a moment of shame or societal judgement that affected me. I loved the father of my children, we just never got married. I had my own business, I set my own income level and chose my own work-hours and now, I owned property. I was a woman who voted and had the freedom to support myself financially. Being in a relationship was a choice, not a necessity for survival. Not a single element of that was easily available a couple of hundred years before. I felt like I was quite literally living the imagined dream of the powerful and passionate women who came before me and who fought for the rights that were now my normal. I felt gratitude for the farmers and creative people who made my food, clothing and furniture possible. I felt such appreciation for my senses, thankful for all I'd seen, heard, smelt, touched, tasted and sensed; what a rich life I had already lived, when viewed from this frame of reference. [Later, I created an affirmation song called, "So Grateful, So Thankful" that you may want to check out if gratitude for basic, daily life is something you would like support with]. Committing to the internal focus of Gratitude FM, opened my mind and heart to seeing and feeling the wonders in my life, rather than what I could have chosen to focus on. If you practice resentment daily, you'll become an expert at seeing reasons for it everywhere. If you practice appreciating beauty, you will see that everywhere as well. This is the power of choosing and prioritising an internal focus. You really will get better and better at what you practice and remember, it is a choice. Your unconscious patterns of thought are there due to a whole lot of repetition. You can choose today to repetitively direct your mental focus in a new way, that can become your easily-accessed frame of reference, with enough practice.

For more external and practical changes, we need to look at how we prioritise our time. If you are someone who really values structure, and already has a daily, weekly and monthly schedule then go ahead and carve out time and space for the practical change you've decided to prioritise. If your investigation into 'what you would cancel over what' yielded clear insights into your most important values, then swap some activities out for others. If you're not so scheduled in your private life, remember to keep your newly-prioritised activity in the front of your mind. If it's a daily commitment to something, make sure it's done before the end of your day or link it with another daily practice. Think of the things you already do each day, like getting out of bed, brushing your teeth or finishing dinner. When we link our new commitment to an existing daily activity, you dramatically increase the likelihood of absorbing it into your new 'normal'.

If you need a few hours a week of this new priority, think though your regular activities and choose the day or days that it will most easily fit. Also, make a note to review and see how it's all working. After a couple of weeks, if you have not made time for this value to be part of your life, then you are going to have to embrace a more intentional structure. Or, if you've made time for it, but it caused you to miss other important things, the review will help you sort through what's not working. For example, you may have made time for those painting classes, or 30 minutes at the gym each day, but there's no food in the house and you haven't done any clothes washing. The pebbles and sand in your jar need time allocation, too!

It is time for you to make some choices.

Journal invitation:

What are you going to prioritise?

What kind of time would you like to devote to this?

Are you willing to be flexible on the time you give? If it is a case of the more hours you give it, the faster you'll have your result, then when would you like this result by? If you extend the timeline for completion, allowing for less hours per week allocated, how does that feel? Is there something to compromise on in the short term for this longer-term goal? Or does it feel alright for the value to come into being in the longer term, working around short-term necessities?

If it requires a change in regular schedule, what can you modify or alter?

If you need to co-ordinate with other people to make this possible, when will you talk with them and formulate a plan?

***

Just like your care label changes with the ages and stages of your life, your priorities will also change and be effected by external events. This list of immediate priorities is not cast in stone. In fact, when you come up with your list, I want you to make a note to check in with yourself in a week from now and then again in a month. Part of being at 'cause', is listening to your body and making it a priority to review how things are working. An essential part of living at 'cause', is asking yourself review questions like these: Is what I'm doing achieving the result I was aiming for? Is it moving me closer or further away from my intended outcome? If I'm not sure yet, as they're hasn't been enough time to really see, then how long am I going to give it? Then make another commitment to review it towards the end of your decided time.

When it's not that simple

When our lives are not following our care label, when we are in conditions that we cannot thrive in, one of the first priorities really needs to be a remedy of that situation. Assessing our priorities is one of the key areas that highlights habitual patterns of living at 'effect'. This is where you will come up against a lot of 'shoulds' that are potentially not of your own, conscious making. This is where limiting decisions that feel immovably real and true will be highlighted. This is also the part of your Happiness Recipe journey where your care label, embodiment of your truth and understanding of your core values will come to be pricelessly useful. Sometimes there's also work that needs to be done on your levels of self-worth and the internal-permission to consider yourself, as well others. Depending on what you've trained those around you to expect, it can feel like a shocking slap in the face to them when you decide that *you* get to be in the mix of people whose needs you prioritise. One of the amazing skills of the human mind is how easily we habituate to new conditions. If you move homes to somewhere with a lot of traffic noise, it doesn't take long before your unconscious mind understands that it's not important enough to give conscious attention to. Kind of like you only pay attention to how often you're blinking if someone mentions it or something gets in your eye. Carry on with life and soon enough, that will stop getting your conscious attention because it is a constant that we've gotten used to. I have supported clients in making huge changes in the way they allocate their attention and communicate in their relationships and I promise, it does become the new 'normal' for everyone. Most of the time, their loved ones appreciate seeing the resulting happiness and enthusiasm and consider the relationship improved. If you are in relationships where the necessary conditions are you having no self-respect and expecting no loving actions in support of what you give, you may choose to make some changes in what you allocate there. My main message with this point is not to live in the self-imposed 'effect' idea that you cannot be who you innately are, because it will upset someone. Bethany Webster said, "I don't owe you a version of me that distracts you from your responsibility to face your own pain" and the simplicity of this is worth sitting with if you are in relationships that are painful. It is not designed to promote nastiness and lack of compassion; giving yourself permission to use your insight to insult people with uninvited commentary, and when they're upset by it, to think, 'that's their problem, not mine'. I share it for those of you who are contorted into emotional positions that are not healthily sustainable, but you're staying in them because it feels easier than dealing with the reactions of the person who wants you to stay that way. I believe that everyone can benefit from coaching, when learning a new skill. When the situations you are in, are precarious, then external support becomes more necessary. Support may be something you choose to prioritise, so you don't feel as though you are charting unnavigated territory alone.

Let's look at some examples of complex, priority-rearranging.

Career and job roles comes up a lot in my 1-1 coaching practice. I have seen a disconnect between care label, values and job role in many and various ways. It may be that the company's product, service or management culture is out of alignment with your values. It may be that the number of hours you are devoting to work necessitates absence in other parts of your life. Perhaps that is not working for you right now due to some immediate situation, or in the long-term, due to other parts of your life that you wish to foster. It may be that you are an intelligent person in a role that is not utilising your capacity. It may be that you are a creative person, in a role that requires robotic formula and where creativity is unacceptable. It may be that you love your job but due to the poor pay, only your most basic needs are being met. It may be that you went into a job or into study for your job as a teenager and have remained on that trajectory ever since, without considering your personality or changed needs and aspirations. It may be that your values and priorities have changed and you've outgrown where you are and desire the next steps in your career. There are countless reasons and these are just some of them.

In many cases, some study or re-training is necessary to move out of dissatisfying circumstances. This could mean that, in the short-term, your income goes down or that you spend less time in other parts of your life while you prioritise this change. Being consciously out of values alignment in the short-term to achieve values alignment in the long-term is very different to not having a long-term plan.

I have worked with many clients to successfully navigate this. One, Glen, did a year-long, night school qualification that allowed him to start his own business, using his heart and mind to help people in a way he hadn't seen possible while working really long hours in his menial, boring job. He and his wife both worked full time, so they discussed how they, as a team, would make this 'extra' space, based on the hours he'd calculated that he'd need. They decided he would study four nights a week, do a half day on either Saturday or Sunday, depending on their other plans, and do a bit less around the house. They committed to a date night to make that one weekday they had together very special. On that night they cooked together, talked together and in the warmer weather, sat outside and enjoyed their garden together and then retired to bed at the same time. Prior to studying, they didn't prioritise nights like this in the same way. This date night rekindled fun and effort for togetherness that had been missing. My client was also a lot happier, knowing he was on the road to using his heart and mind in his work, and living in alignment with his care label and values. He had a spring in his step and aliveness in his being that brought new chemistry to their relationship as well. Had he told his wife what he was doing and just announced that he'd be cooking less, doing less around the house and working on his career, it would not have gone as well. When we communicate and plan together, acknowledging that time together is precious and important and openly value and communicate appreciation for the support in your life, great change is possible.

Glen was referred to me, by a medical doctor, with depression he'd suffered with for over five years. He had been unable to see any light looking forward into his future. How he felt when he talked about doing his job for another thirty years because "it was all he knew how to do" was like filling the room with heavy lead. The light in his being turned on as soon as there was a plan, and shone brighter still when he got the results back from his first assignment. He was seeing his capacity in a way he'd never seen it in high school!

In this example of 'not so simple' priority changes, there were many options. This course was available as an intensive. An option was to quit his job and study full time, finishing sooner and starting his business earlier. It was in prioritising the financial reward of working full time, and sacrificing hours usually spent in other ways that this way forward was forged. Sometimes, clients will sacrifice financial 'extras' for a period of retraining, knowing that there will be an increase in financial benefit once requalified. It will always depend on your care label, values and other life circumstances, to find what is right for you. In Australia, where I live, Universities allow ten years to complete a three-year degree, which allows for part time study while also working and/or parenting. There are on-line and in-person options which will also suit different people for their own reasons. When we sit at 'cause' and ask the questions around, "What *could* I do?" and "What *is* possible here?", new options open up to prioritise the change you desire.

I had another client, Jennifer, who wanted to lose weight, gain back her fitness and flexibility and feel great within herself, like she had before motherhood. She came to me with the 'truth' that there was just no time for this, as she was fully booked up with other commitments. She worked during the hours her four children were at school and was the primary carer for all day to day activities and family needs. She did all the housework, cooking and life administration, like managing the finances. She was a very big believer in supporting her children's interests and all four of her children played a sport, an instrument and had at least one other activity that had a weekly, in-person time commitment. There were other 'truths' that were contributing to Jennifer having virtually no time for herself. The big one was, 'No one will help me'. This included her children and husband, who were not contributing around the house, and also her local family and friends. Initially, when she had first begun her motherhood adventure, doing everything for her children and her husband felt wonderful. It gave her an identity she liked, she felt empowered, caring and loving. By the time she invested in working with me, she had children ranging from eight to 15 years old. It no longer felt wonderful that she did all the shopping, made all the meals and then had five, able-bodied people, sitting and relaxing, not even watching her also do all the cleaning up. Before seeing me, she would ask, "Can someone please help me with this?" and everyone would have something else to do, that she allowed them to prioritise, like "No, I've got homework" or "Oh, I really need some downtime, I'll help you later". And that help never happened. To cut a long story short, we did a lot of inner and outer work! We worked on reframing her motherhood role. She began to see that part of being a loving parent was preparing her children for adult life, where they would need skills to look after themselves and understand how to be part of a partnership or group. If she continued the way she had, none of them would leave home with cooking, cleaning or life management skills. None of them would move in with other people with the understanding of their part in the whole and a healthy work ethic around contributing. All the children got household jobs. Not to 'help her', but as the expected contribution. Most human beings of any age experience a bit of resistance when conditions change, just like you have resisted some of the changes you have decided to make for yourself. It's normal. Jennifer understood this, framed it up as the new 'normal', and that is exactly what it became. She also spoke to the other parents she knew, from all the activities she watched her children do each week, and became a ring-leader for some positive changes for everyone. For each activity, she organised a car pool so each parent only had to attend the activity once every four weeks. When it was her turn, she was fully present and her children looked forward to her being there. It became special and appreciated, rather than expected. She had a pivotal conversation with her husband about how much their lives had changed since parenthood. She honoured him and all the hours he put into work to provide for them all. She also honoured herself and asked him to reconnect to her, the woman, outside of her caring roles. They became more of a working-together team, rather than divided into separate job roles. They made some financial decisions and committed to a long-term strategy that honoured the short-term situation as well. They stopped living by default and broke the mould that wasn't really exciting for either of them. The changes she made, by being coached to listen to her own, innate wisdom, her frustrations and dissatisfactions, changed the entire family for the betterment of everyone.

What can get in the way - Freeing up time

Sometimes, it's not a matter of needing a transformational epiphany to happen, or relationship-changing conversations. It can just be a matter of really looking at what the time leaks are in your habitual life. Often it is the activities that we are so used to doing, that we don't think to ask the warehouse of our incredible wisdom, "How could I be doing this differently?" Often, the more in 'the blurk' we are, the less creative we even think of being. Things feel heavy and hard and so they just keep being that way. You have amazing power for transforming your life, when you ask yourself different questions. When we ask, "Why is it so hard?" and "Why am I the only one who does all this?", your resources will give you answers that keep adding to those blurky feelings. When we choose to shift into, "What is happening that I'm really enjoying?", "What needs to change?", "How can I make this simpler and easier?", "Who can I team up with?", "How can I do this differently?" then your resources can get to work answering those things.

I often get my clients to write down ten new ways that they could do or organise one of their time-leaks differently. When you need to come up with a big list, and you're not really invested in the answers, you can come up with some wackier solutions that may be the answer or part of the answer. We need to get out of our mental ruts to see new ways of doing things. The answers are often, quite outside of the box.

Here are some common time-leaks and some suggestions:

Basic meal-planning and shopping only once a week.

Many clients spend a lot of time food shopping, popping back to the shops for meal ingredients many times through the week. If the idea of planning a week of meals makes you feel restricted and boring, then just some 'meal imagining' is fine. With some longer-shelf-life staples you can keep in the cupboard, there is a huge variety of meals you can put together with the same, fresh ingredients.

Using your time while driving for other activities.

Obviously, I mean safe and legal activities! How can you use your time in the car in ways that feel great? If you wish that you had more time to talk with your friends and family, dial them up before you leave and chat while you drive. If you wish you had more time to read for fun and interest, see which of your favourite authors have created audiobooks and receive their words and stories while you drive. I have had many A-Grade/High Distinction students who use their time driving to listen to their lectures or study material. They already had the habit of listening several times to each one, and this car-listen created more time for the other types of study techniques that ensured their high-level grades.

Asking for help or mutually-beneficial exchange.

Like the older-style of living in a village, receiving and offering support from those around you can create a wonderful feeling of caring community. It also frees up time for you, and for others, too! Car-pooling for your children's activities so you have less in-person hours committed is one idea. Looking after other people's children as an exchange for them looking after yours is another. If you find it difficult to ask for help or suggest an exchange, then please ask yourself what you value more. If the answer is being seen as someone who never asks for help, then keep on going. If you would like to include more of your core values in your life, and need to prioritise them, then I suggest learning this skill of asking for mutually beneficial exchanges. If you ask someone who, you know, also struggles with asking for assistance, you're offering both of you a great, growth opportunity.

Remember that the decision for the inclusion of your core values into your priorities, is an ongoing exploration. You are entering a process of trial and correction. See what works and what doesn't. Change can be a bit uncomfortable, because it is new and therefore unknown. Your inner congruency may be a "Yes!", but the new ways of doing this, out in your life, are untried. It is okay to feel a bit hesitant or unsure. Dip your toes into these new waters. Be mindful of your care label. Take your time and embrace curiosity as you try new things. You are *so* worthy of this effort and you are the only one that can do it. No one else can feel into your congruency for you. In the hands of others, your priorities will be matching *their* care label. So, don't feel alone in it, feel empowered by all the control you have to choose your priorities, both internally and externally.

Conclusion

"I was blessed because I was loved by you."

- Celine Dion

So many of us love 'love'. We know that great love has the power to heal and transform lives. We cry happy tears at weddings where the couple truly adore, fully accept and bring out the best in each other. It moves us when we see great friends, in their older years, talking about the love and support that has been shared throughout their lives. What I want you to imagine, when reading the Celine Dion quote above, is the blessing you can give your own life when you choose to love and care for yourself. Not the ideal of yourself that someone else values. Not the You, you hope to one day be. The You that you are, right now. It is only in this very moment that you have the power to affect your life and to build in the changes that lead, with practice, to that You, you hope to one day be.

We have spent this book exploring all the start-up ingredients you need. The first is the acknowledgment of your own individuality. Just look at any family with multiple children. They may have the same parents and basic upbringing, but will all have totally distinct personalities, likes and dislikes. What drains and discourages them will be different. What enlivens and inspires them will be different, too. Knowing that each person is unique, and therefore is entitled to have differing needs, wants and interests, can eliminate judgments and evoke curiosity. You have a uniqueness that makes you, You. Working *with* your own nature is the only road to real and lasting confidence and sustainable, healthy happiness.

"Confidence is the practical form of being true to one's own consciousness"

- Ayn Rand

There are two types of happiness. The Surface and the Soul-Deep. Please don't, ever again, fall into the trap of believing they are the same thing and rob yourself of true and lasting self-acceptance and contentment. Pretending that the surface can represent the soul is a denial of your depth; a disconnection between your essence, from where all inspiration flows, and your practical life experience. It's like having amazing fuel for a super car in a locked room of your house, that has no relationship to the garage or to your vehicle. Your essence, living within and around your body, is impotent if you ignore or supress its feedback about your life. It can be your greatest and most competent ally if you allow yourself to be whole. Wholefully and soulfully, You.

Your internal dialog is powerful. You can be like a debilitating and confidence-shattering manager that stands over your own shoulder, micro-managing everything you do with negative commentary about how sub-standard you are. You can also choose to manage yourself within a framework of self-acceptance, goal-setting and actions toward achievement in the areas you wish to improve. You can choose to regularly review, so as to adjust what's not working and engage in intentional, internal commentary about what you are doing well. You get to choose what you practice. Your thoughts create your feelings, and your feelings flood your body with chemicals. You are the driver of this process. To paraphrase, Dr Joe Dispenza you can break the habit of being your 'old self' and cultivate a new way of being; a new You. It requires getting into 'cause', casting off in a new self-honouring direction, and taking the daily actions to hardwire new neural pathways. In doing this, you will, in time, have new, unconscious reactions to things. You will become the You, you used to dream of being. Every single step of this is in your hands. No one can think for you. No one can feel for you. No one else has any control over your own free will, once you are an adult. Claim this adulthood for yourself and the freedom you have to direct your focus.

You were born with a care label, but it is not printed on your skin anywhere. This creates the need for self-reflection and inquiry; for trial and correction, practical application and review. Be so proud of yourself that you're putting time into this. I promise it will empower you and change your life, in every area you choose to apply it. Getting to know yourself and the conditions *you* need to thrive is one of life's greatest adventures and most rewarding journeys of your life.

Please know that the real metamorphosis happens as you apply these tools. No tool can change your life without application. Owning a chainsaw doesn't mean we know how to use it. New ideas can spark new desires for life-changes but to create real change, as we have explored in these pages, we need to address repetitive and well-practiced thoughts and behaviours. If we always do what we've always done, we will keep on getting, more or less, the same kinds of things we've always had. This is one of the traps of ongoing personal development. Looking for the 'next thing' that will make all the difference, without really putting to use the tools already learned. It is the application and the new verbs you action that bring the new results into your life experience. So, with this book, I wholeheartedly celebrate you for reading it. I encourage you to get some personalised support if you need to. Listen to your body's wisdom. It will know. Apply the tools before moving on to the next lot of learning. If it all stays only in the realm of conceptual ideas, without entering your practical being as new thoughts, new choices, new behaviours and new priorities that are values-aligned, then you will not be getting from this book what it has to offer. Having or reading the book won't make the changes. The internet is full of recipes, and so are the cookbooks most of us have, but we can still get stuck with no ideas about what to make for dinner. That's totally okay, we all go there. True empowerment, and living at 'cause', is knowing you don't have to stay there. You can choose to use the recipe you now have.

You are unique and you are powerful. You have on-board, embodied wisdom and ways of listening to it, to guide your life in a fully-congruent direction. You now know of your Happiness Recipe and how important it is. It makes my heart so joyful to think of you, knowing your care label and using your Recipe to guide your one-of-a-kind life.

With smiles from my heart to yours and in celebration of the uniqueness you bring to the world we currently share, I end this part of our journey together. Wishing you every happiness that is the result of you, loving yourself enough, to give yourself the conditions that enliven and support the fullest expression of Beautiful You.

www.ieshadelune.com

9 781645 166559